LOOKING IN THE MIRROR

SELF-APPRAISAL IN THE LOCAL CHURCH

Lyle E. Schaller

• *Illustrated by Edward Lee Tucker* •

ABINGDON PRESS · Nashville

LOOKING IN THE MIRROR
Self-Appraisal in the Local Church

Copyright © 1984 by Abingdon Press

Fifth Printing 1986

Library of Congress Cataloging in Publication Data

SCHALLER, LYLE E.
    Looking in the mirror.
    Bibliography: p.
    1. Church management.   I. Title.
    BV652.S325   1984   254   83-15857

ISBN 0-687-22635-X

MANUFACTURED BY THE PARTHENON PRESS AT
NASHVILLE, TENNESSEE, UNITED STATES OF AMERICA

To
Donald L. Houser
Frederick A. Marks
W. Baxter Weant
Martin L. Yonts

Contents

Introduction

"It's one thing to sit in your living room and look at pictures of alligators in the *National Geographic*. It's another thing to be waist deep in swamp water in Florida!" declared the minister in his second year of developing a new congregation in Georgia. The subject under discussion was whether a proposed training event for ministers organizing new congregations should be designed for pastors *before* they were assigned as mission developers or for ministers who had three to six months behind them in their call to create a new congregation. The speaker was arguing for the second alternative.

This book is not about organizing new congregations, but it is designed for congregational leaders both lay and clergy who sometimes feel they are waist deep in swamp water and surrounded by alligators. In part it is an attempt to help the reader understand why alligators flourish in certain places, but are rarely found in most of the swampland on this continent. In other words, this book is directed at the practitioners who are out attempting to drain the swamps, not at the observers who occasionally share in corporate worship when they are not watching television, but who are not otherwise actively engaged in the life, ministry, pain, outreach, and struggles of the worshiping congregation.

This book rests on three basic assumptions. The first goes back to Plato's admonition in *Apology*, "…the unexamined life is not worth living." Both the Old Testament and the New Testament contain scores of declarations that every child of God should be engaged in self-appraisal. That concept is central to the Christian practice of confession and seeking forgiveness. It is only a short step beyond that to the concept of corporate self-appraisal. In other words, it is assumed that it is appropriate, productive, and good for congregational leaders periodically to engage themselves in the process of appraising the role, ministry, internal dynamics,

9

outreach, and life of that congregation. Like many other areas of human endeavor, there is the danger of overindulgence with a resulting "paralysis from analysis," but every worthwhile venture includes risks. This book is intended to offer a conceptual framework for this process of congregational self-appraisal.

The second basic assumption is that (a) if people can agree on the larger context, it will be easier to agree on details and (b) if people have the benefit of a reasonably accurate diagnosis of reality, they can be more effective than many of them believe in solving the problem or in living with the ambiguity that is present when a problem does not have a neat solution or in resolving diversionary or destructive conflict.

The first four chapters represent an attempt to offer four different systems for looking at congregations. Not everyone will find every chapter speaking to the condition of every congregation. For example, some readers may find it easy to decide whether their congregation resembles a cat or a collie or a garden or a ranch as described in the first chapter, but may not be able to decide whether it is predominantly a second-person church or predominantly a Bible-centered church to use the conceptual framework offered in the fourth chapter. The sole purpose of the classification systems offered in these four chapters is to help the reader develop a conceptual framework that will explain contemporary reality more clearly. If one of these classification systems does not fit your congregation, please do not worry about it. Simply turn to the next chapter. Perhaps that next chapter will speak to your efforts at self-appraisal.

The third of the three assumptions that provide the foundation for this volume is that self-appraisal and information can be a key factor in overcoming the apathy and passivity that blight so many congregations. This book is based on a central assertion of information theory—that order and sense can prevail against disorder and nonsense.[1] This writer not only believes in God as the creator, but also believes God was and is an orderly creator. This is not a random or ad hoc world in which we live. While there are dangers in an excessive emphasis on a logical, rational, and businesslike approach to the church (that is the thesis of the second chapter), this book affirms the idea that a comprehensive classification system can be a very useful tool in self-appraisal and planning. Sense and order are compatible with a Christian doctrine of creation.

Another way of introducing the reader to this book is to explain first what it is not and next what it is. This is not a book on the Christian faith. It is based on the values and teachings of the Christian faith, but it is not a book about the faith. It assumes the church is a community which nourishes the faith of the members, but this volume is not directed at the personal and spiritual journey of the individual Christian. It is about the corporate life of the worshiping community, but it is not a book about worship.

This book represents an attempt to look at congregational life from nontraditional and nonconventional perspectives. This point can be illustrated by three other books published in recent years. In 1975 Edward O. Wilson's book *Sociobiology: The New Synthesis* (Harvard University Press) broke new ground in helping us understand human behavior. [2] A second example is the impact of Walter Wink's *The Bible in Human Transformation* has had in helping us understand the central reason for studying the Bible. [3] We study the Bible to know, understand, and reinforce our faith as Christians. The third example is Paul Colinvaux's *The Fates of Nations* [4] in which the author offers an ecological analysis of military history. While none of these books offers a complete analysis of the subject under discussion, each book helps us broaden our understanding of contemporary reality by looking at the subject from a fresh perspective. That is the purpose of this volume. It is intended to offer congregational leaders several different perspectives in their efforts at the appraisal of that church.

To a limited extent the approach followed in this book parallels that used by Donald A. Schon in *The Reflective Practitioner*. [5] The contents of this book are based on thirty years of firsthand observations of what is happening in the churches, rather than from scholarly research or controlled experiments. That can be a useful approach to identifying reality.

By the time they reach the last chapter some readers may be curious about the omission of chapters on the self-appraisal of such traditional programmatic areas as worship, education, missions, social action, and evangelism. There are three reasons for these omissions. The most obvious is that this would increase the length of the book by at least one hundred pages, and some readers will agree it is already too fat.

More important, the distinctive purpose of this volume is to lift up concepts in congregational self-appraisal that have not been covered in other books. Hundreds of books have been published in recent years discussing these programmatic concerns. The primary focus of this volume is to lift up questions and issues that often are neglected in the traditional approaches to congregational self-appraisal. That is the reason for the inclusion of chapters on membership trends, youth ministries, the weekday nursery school, and the building planning committee. In each of these chapters, as well as in the rest of the book, the emphasis has been on considerations that frequently are overlooked.

Finally, this is not intended to be a comprehensive self-study manual. Scores of these have been published during the past three decades. The central goal of his book is to help congregational leaders expand their conceptual framework and ask new questions in self-appraisal efforts.

This book is directed at those church members, both lay and clergy, who enjoy thinking on the reflective or analytical level. Each chapter is intended to stimulate the reader to reflect on the life of the church from a new perspective. For example, the first chapter questions the conventional wisdom of those who advocate the merger of small membership churches. Can you create a collie by merging two cats? Will the union of a cat and a big collie produce a garden? In other words, the reader is invited to playfully reflect on the points raised here and not to take the contents as a rigid set of guidelines.

In broad general terms this volume consists of three sections. The first four chapters raise broad general questions about the distinctive nature of the worshiping congregation. Does your church resemble a garden or a ranch? Do the leaders try to "run it like a business?" Is it primarily legalistic or ideological or behavioral in character? Which person of the Trinity receives special emphasis?

The next seven chapters focus in more on various aspects of congregational life ranging from the turning points of the past to the characteristics of today's members to the conceptual framework for program planning.

The last three chapters raise questions that frequently are overlooked about three specific aspects of congregational life.

In each chapter, however, the central point is to raise questions that will help leaders in their efforts at congregational self-appraisal. When your church looks into the mirror, what do you see? These questions may sharpen up the image you see in your self-appraisal effort.

1

CATS, COLLIES, AND RANCHES

"For the past two years I've been trying to persuade the small congregation I serve out in the country to cooperate in programming with the church in town where I also am the minister," commented Tom Parsons who was in his third year as the pastor of this two-church parish. "With the exception of last summer, when we had a joint vacation Bible school, I've had no luck. I can't understand why the folks out in the country don't want to cooperate. The members of my church in town are so open to the idea of the two congregations cooperating in program."

"One of my biggest frustrations is that we haven't been able to get the leaders from our really small churches to come to our training programs," sighed the executive minister of a regional judicatory. "We've had some top-notch training events for our smaller congregations, but the folks from our smallest churches rarely come out."

"I hate to go away for more than three or four days at a time," complained Virginia Burke, the pastor of a congregation averaging 150 people at Sunday morning worship. "Whenever I'm gone for a longer period, there is so much work piled up for me when I get back that it takes the fun out of the trip. All I think about is that mountain of work that is accumulating while I'm away."

These three comments point up the first question that should be asked in the congregation where the members are engaged in a process of self-examination. Who are we? What are our distinctive characteristics as a congregation? What distinguishes this congregation from other churches?

One part of that unique local identity grows out of the origins, heritage, and traditions of that congregation. Another part is a product of the community context. A third component often can be traced back to the imprint of one or two long pastorates.

Another set of clues to help us understand who we are and why we behave as we do can be gleaned from the review of the differences among churches that are an outgrowth of size.

A useful frame of reference is to think in terms of a classification system, rather than simply to compare congregations with one another.[1] The classification system suggested here uses seven analogies to help us picture the differences among churches.

Have You Ever Owned a Cat?

Approximately one-hundred-thousand Protestant[2] congregations in the United States and Canada average fewer than thirty-five people in attendance at the principal weekly worship service. Together these very small congregations account for more than one-fourth of all Protestant congregations on the North American continent and for approximately 5 percent of all Protestant churchgoers on the typical Sabbath.

It may help us to understand the distinctive characteristics of these congregations if we liken them to a cat. Have you ever owned a cat? If you answer yes, you do not understand cats. No one *owns* a cat! You may keep a cat. You may work for a cat. You may have taken care of a wandering cat who came to live with you. You may have a cat in your house as a pet. You may have a cat as a landlord, but you do not *own* a cat. Cats are very independent creatures. Cats are self-sufficient. Cats take care of themselves. Cats do not like to be dependent on others. Cats have powerful instincts that direct their behavior patterns. The female cat instinctively knows how to be a good mother to that litter of hungry kittens. No one has to develop a training program to teach that four-legged mother how to take care of her kittens.

The really small congregation displays many of the characteristics of a cat. These churches, which we can label as "fellowships," resemble an overgrown group more than they resemble the popular stereotype of what a full-blown church should be. Together they constitute a distinctive category in our classification system. Together they account for one-fourth of all Protestant churches on this continent.

For decades the experts in denominational circles have been predicting the demise of many of these fellowships. Folklore proclaims that cats have nine lives. So do most of these very small

Average Attendance...
AT
WORSHIP·TYPE ...
·ANALOGY

fewer than 35	fellowship	cat
35-100	small church	collie
100-175	middle-sized	garden
175-225	awkward size	house
225-450	large	mansion
450-700	huge	ranch
700 and more	mini-denomi-nation	nation

churches. They can be yoked with a larger church, but they survive. Thousands have survived some of the worst mistakes and poorest sermons of the most inept of the apprentice preachers. Many have survived the determined efforts of denominational leaders to close them. They can survive decades of neglect, abuse, and mistreatment.

The vacancy between the departure of one resident minister and the arrival of the successor may be as long as two or three years, but the fellowship church does not appear to suffer any serious negative effects of this neglect. Cats do not like to be dependent on others.

Frequently one hears a minister refer to "my church," but the possessive term rarely can be applied to these fellowships. They do not belong to any preachers. They are independent and self-sufficient. No one owns a cat. No preacher owns these fellowships. That minister may care for the fellowship, may even regard it as a favorite pet and may feed it spiritually, but that pastor does not own it.

"No one ever gets on top of a cat!"
——FRIAR TUCK

The staff of the regional judicatory often complain that these fellowships do not express a strong sense of denominational identity. They forget that cats are independent creatures and rarely wear anyone's family name.

Likewise the denominational executive, who is upset when representatives from the fellowships seldom attend those training events for people from small churches, should understand that cats rarely are seeking someone to train them. The cat's behavior pattern is a product of instinct, not training. Cats rarely seek advice on how to improve their behavior patterns. Readers who have tried to train a cat can understand why members from these fellowships tend to ignore denominational training programs. Cats do not voluntarily enroll in training schools! Cats already know the answers to all the questions they believe are relevant.

Some of the clergy have considerable practice in making declarations that begin with the words, "Every church should . . ." These ministers gain some useful insights into reality by talking with human beings who declare, "Cats should be trained not to jump up on the table while we are eating." The word "should" has little relevance to most discussions about the training of cats. For example, it is not uncommon to hear the declaration, "Every little church ought to plan to grow into a bigger congregation!" Have you ever encountered a cat that wanted to be transformed into a dog? We can gain some additional insights into the behavior of these fellowship churches as we look at several other categories in this classification system.

Isn't That a Friendly Collie?

More than one-third of all Protestant churches on the North American continent average between thirty-five and a hundred people at their principle weekly worship service. In this classification system these congregations can be likened to collies. Collies come in different sizes. Some are big dogs. Some are relatively small. Occasionally one will encounter a mean dog that has been abused by a previous owner, but almost all collies are affectionate creatures. They enjoy being loved and they return the affection.[3] Collies are responsive to sensitive human beings and can be trained to respond to external expectations that run counter to the dog's natural instincts. Many self-identified enablers among the clergy enjoy serving these small churches because they receive a favorable and affirming response to their efforts as trainers.

Denominational leaders appreciate collies because many of them respond to the training events planned for leaders from small churches. (Have you ever seen a cat willingly participate in a training event designed for dogs?) When they leave, many of them lavishly express their appreciation for what happened.

Collie

"A little love goes a long way with a large dog."

— FRIAR TUCK

When the pastor of the collie-sized church returns from a two-or three-week vacation or from several days at a continuing education event, that minister usually receives a warm reception and finds little has changed during his or her absence. (When the resident of a house that includes a cat returns, it often is a bit disconcerting to be ignored by the cat, who appears to be unaware that you have been gone and is more interested in being fed.)

In thousands of communities one minister serves a two-church parish that includes a friendly collie and an aloof cat displaying little interest in going to visit the collie on the dog's turf or in socializing with dogs. (There are exceptions to that generalization. We have a neutered tomcat whose mother was a long-haired alley cat and whose father was a teddy bear that loves to go out and romp with a fourteen-year-old schnauzer who lives next door. However, he regards every other dog as a natural enemy.)

The pastor of the two-church circuit that includes a cat and a collie traditionally has been advised, "It's important that you treat both the same way. Be sure not to favor one congregation over the other." Better advice would be, "Remember, cats and dogs are different! Be sure to treat the cat like a cat, not a dog. Likewise the key factor with the collie will be to shower it with affection." Some people wonder why these small churches tend to remain on a plateau in size or why church shoppers often do not return after that initial visit. Collies tend to have a strong affection for members of the family, but they often bark at strangers.

Most people enjoy collies and on the typical Sunday in 1984 an estimated eight million Protestant churchgoers attended worship in a collie-sized congregation. Collies account for somewhat more than one-third of all Protestant congregations and for slightly less than one-fifth of all Protestant churchgoers on the North American continent.

A more cynical observer of this process once declared, "No, what it really resembles is the institutional tendency to throw the new seminary graduates to the dogs."
—FRIAR TUCK

One of the more subtle changes in the dynamics of small membership churches in recent years can be traced back to the changing source of pastors. During the first half of this century thousands of young men who went into the pastoral ministry were drawn from among the children who had grown up in rural America and were nurtured in small membership churches. Typically their first ministerial assignment was to a cat or collie-size congregation, or perhaps to a yoked arrangement that consisted of a cat and a collie. That posed no problems since the new minister carried many years of firsthand recollections of the dynamics and congregational life-style of that size church. He knew the characteristics of the cat and the collie.

During the past three or four decades, however, an increasing proportion of persons going into the ministry have come from much larger congregations. Many have had no firsthand contact with a congregation of fewer than six or seven hundred members. Frequently their first ministerial responsibility, following graduation from seminary, is to serve as the pastor of a collie-size congregation. This can be a difficult experience for both the new pastor and the parishioners. Occasionally the new minister feels rejected. The pattern is the same as when the body of a heart transplant recipient tends to reject that new organ. There is a natural tendency for a body to reject what it perceives as a foreign or alien object. A more cynical observer of this process once declared, "No, what it really resembles is the institutional tendency to throw the new seminary graduates to the dogs."

The Gardener's Work Is Never Done

Another 15 percent of the Protestant churches on this continent average between 100 and 175 at worship. For the most part the 50,000 to 60,000 congregations in this category are very unlike smaller churches. To represent this discontinuity we move out of the animal kingdom to choose an analogy. These middle-sized churches resemble a garden. Some gardens are much larger than others. Some gardens have the benefit of rich and fertile soil. Others are located in barren ground. Most of the churches in this category need, can afford, and do have the services of a full-time resident minister, although several thousand share a pastor with a collie or a cat.

From the ministerial perspective this classification evokes several reflections on reality.

It is much easier to look after two or three cats or a cat and a collie than to take care of two gardens.

A Gardener's
Work Is Never Done'

Many churches of this type
share a fulltime minister
with a collie or a cat (GULP!)

—FRIAR TUCK

The gardener's work is never done. If the gardener is away from home for several days, the neglect is very obvious when that gardener returns. Usually there is considerable work awaiting the gardener's return. In some seasons of the year this is a more severe problem than in others.

While there are natural forces that limit how large a cat or a collie can become, a garden can be greatly increased in size without any radical changes in character. Growth on a large scale means more work for the gardener, and it may be necessary to employ some part-time help, but gardens respond to the concept of quantitative growth more comfortably than do cats and dogs. Eventually, however, the garden may grow to the point that it would be more realistic to refer to it as a truck farm or a ranch than to continue to limit one's thinking by seeing it as a garden. When that happens, of course, the basic responsibilities of the gardener are transformed.

It also means a new and radically different organizational structure for managing the big gardens. In addition, the truck farm is less dependent on volunteers who work in the garden in their spare time and increasingly dependent on an organized and disciplined paid work force. This often is easier for the new owner to understand than it is for the person who started that garden on a small plot of land twenty years ago.

The garden demands most of the gardener's time and it certainly is helpful to have someone available to answer the telephone while the gardener is out in the field.

The collie wants to love and be loved. The garden needs someone who loves gardens, but is willing and able to accept a leadership role in planning and decision-making, and who has the ability to think in a longer time frame than either the cat or collie believe is necessary. Cats and collies live in today's world, but the garden is dependent on someone who can plan at least one season in advance. The enabler or trainer may be remarkably effective when working with the collie, but the garden needs someone who is willing to take charge.

While some readers may have difficulty believing this, several Protestant denominations operate on the assumption that the best training for a future gardener is to spend several years working with cats and collies.

Finally, several young ministers have complained that the theological school they attended trained them to serve as gardeners, but offered little preparation in the care of cats and dogs.

Why Use This System?

At this point it is appropriate to suggest a half-dozen reasons why this classification system is being used as the opening chapter in a book on congregational self-appraisal.

First, and most obvious, this series of categories emphasizes the discontinuity as churches are classified by size. The congregation averaging twenty people at worship is not a miniature version of the congregation that includes one hundred at worship. They are different orders of creation.

Second, when a congregation moves from one size bracket to another, it also changes some of its basic characteristics. When long-time members say, "It's not like it used to be," they are correct in their appraisal. It is different.

Third, when a minister moves from serving as the pastor of a two-church parish composed of a cat and a collie to a congregation of 150 to 160 at worship, that move results in more than a change of address. It also means a radical change in the ministerial role for that pastor. The gifts and skills that are necessary and appropriate for taking care of cats and dogs are not the same as the gifts and skills required of an effective gardener.

Fourth, the form of oversight and discipline that needs to be exercised in the care of a collie is not the same as for a cat or a garden. Likewise the system of church government that is appropriate for one size congregation may not fit another size.

Fifth, the leadership role of the person caring for a cat is different from that of the gardener. In general, the larger the size of a congregation, the greater the pressures on the minister to be an initiating leader and the longer the time frame needed for planning.

Finally, most of us are more comfortable when we are encouraged to think in visual terms. Jesus taught us the value of word pictures in communicating abstract concepts. Most of us can picture in our minds more readily the differences between a cat and a collie than we can the differences between the congregation averaging twenty at worship and the one averaging seventy. Visual imagery helps us understand subtle differences. This point can be illustrated by returning to this classification system and identifying four other categories of churches.

Who Repairs the Plumbing in Your House?

One Protestant church in twenty on this continent averages between 175 and 225 at worship. These churches include one out of nine churchgoers on the typical Sunday morning. Their congregations can be described as "awkward" in size. Most of them are too large to be adequately served by one pastor without the assistance of other program staff, but frequently the leaders are convinced that "we can neither justify nor afford a second minister." These congregations are not quite large enough to fit comfortably into the large church bracket, but they are too big to function effectively as middle-sized congregations. One common characteristic of many churches of this size is that they include a substantial number of inactive members. They often include more people than they are able to accommodate and care for adequately. Others often fluctuate between 220 and 240 at worship when everything is going well, but drop to 160 to 180 at worship when encountering rough seas. Scores of these awkward-size congregations have fluctuated in that range for decades without even being able to move into and institutionalize a permanent place for themselves inside that large church bracket.

In our classification system they resemble a house. Houses, like gardens, come in widely varying sizes, but a house is a different species of creation than a garden. Some houses are far more complex than others. The house includes several specialized rooms such as the bathroom, the kitchen, and the bedrooms. This size church also usually includes specialized ministries with children or mature adults or individuals with special needs. While some new houses do appear to be carbon copies of others, by the time they are twenty years old, it is safe to say no two are alike. Some are rundown and in need of rehabilitation while others have been completely remodeled recently. Some suffer from deferred maintenance while others are in excellent condition. Few congregations in this size category find carbon copies of themselves.

The care of a house requires a different set of skills than are necessary to care for a garden. An excessively frequent turnover in the person in charge of the house often results in an above average pace of deterioration.

One of the distinctive characteristics of a house is that many homeowners rely on outside specialists for help. The list includes plumbers, carpenters, electricians, roofers, and specialists in heating and cooling systems. Likewise this size church often turns to an outsider to direct the choir or lead the youth program or plan a financial campaign or revitalize the Sunday school or carry out some of the parish visitation or oversee some other dimension of parish life. When we move beyond the garden-size congregation, the emphasis increasingly is on specialized skills when discussing staff needs.

From a ministerial perspective the work is never done, surprises frequently emerge that need immediate attention, the specialists who are called in sometimes do not meet expectations and stormy weather can create additional chores. The visitors who come by often are highly impressed, occasionally they display signs of envy, but rarely do they comprehend the amount of lonely work that is required to maintain that old house in such fine condition.

A large proportion of church members, especially those who live in single family homes, find the house-size congregation to be ideal. Everyone knows one another. It is not necessary for people to bother wearing name tags. Kinship ties reinforce congregational cohesion. There are enough volunteers to carry the basic work load. Some of the occasional "fixing up" can be done by volunteers. The members care for one another and emergencies reinforce the sense of belonging. Some new members who are not related to anyone in that house feel it is exclusionary and difficult for a stranger to be accepted.

Those who would like to turn the average house into a mansion must face the fact that such a transformation has several price tags on it. These include more staff, more meeting rooms for more programs, a tolerance of the increased complexity, higher per person operational costs, more parking to accommodate the increased number of people, adaptation to a change in how the rest of the community views it and, most important of all, a determination to pay the price of expansion.

That Is Too Rich for Our Blood!

A slightly broader category of churches consists of those large congregations averaging between 225 and 450 at worship. These large congregations can be likened to a mansion—there is a high degree of discontinuity with the previous category, but also some continuity.

Unlike the garden or the house, the mansion almost always requires directional signs to help strangers find their way around the place. The mansion also requires a larger staff of specialists—a pattern that visitors from the garden often view as a luxury. The mansion is a very complex structure and it may appear that something always needs fixing, but the mansion can accommodate a very large number of people at any one time, although most of them will not be able to call more than a few of the others by name. Events planned for the mansion usually have to be scheduled well in advance, carefully organized and adequately staffed. In the house everyone appears to know everyone else, but anonymity is a mark of the mansion.

The person in charge of the mansion should be a well-organized and personally attractive individual who is comfortable and skilled at building and maintaining relationships with strangers, who knows how to make visitors feel welcome, who is unusually competent at remembering names, and who can work effectively with the large staff required to care for such a big operation.

People passing by often are impressed by the sheer size and impressive appearance of the structure. They may wonder what goes on inside, but most are too shy to walk in on their own initiative. A substantial number are convinced, simply by looking at the building, "That's too rich for my blood," and walk past in their search for a smaller house, an attractive garden or a friendly collie. Some outsiders try to rent the facility for a wedding or some other special ceremony. Some mansions are available for rent. Others are not.

Conversations with long-time residents of a mansion often evoke such comments as: "There was a day when I knew everyone who lived here, but now it seems like most of my old friends are gone and all I see are strangers." Or "If you knew how much it costs to operate this place, you would be amazed." Or "There's more going on here in a week than anyone has time to attend." Or "The help we're able to secure today simply is not up to the quality we had when I moved in here thirty years ago." Or "I can't understand why anyone would want to live in one of those little crackerboxes when they could come here." Or "We really have a broad range of people here tonight; it's not like it used to be when everyone you met here was somebody." Or "It seems like the help is too busy now to even talk with us." Or "I can remember when a lady wore a hat and gloves whenever she came in here!" Or "When our daughter was married here in 1955, it took the workmen three days to decorate; now they run weddings through here like it was Reno." Or "It seems to me there was more going on around here back in the fifties than now, but today we have more staff than we had then. How come?"

Mansion Ministry

"It takes a Super-Preacher-Creature to minister to a mansion!"

—FRIAR TUCK.

The really perceptive occupants of the mansion see no inconsistency in the fact that the residents include three cats and a collie or that many people spend far more time in the garden than in the mansion. In fact, several people identify the gardener as their closest friend on the staff. Some folks see the cats as aloof creatures who refuse to socialize with the rest of the residents, but that is the nature of a cat. The big mansions accept the fact that a few cats and that collie are necessary to make everyone feel comfortable here.

The 35,000 churches in this category account for fewer than 10 percent of all Protestant congregations, but they include nearly one-fourth of all the people at worship on the typical Sabbath.

Who Tends the Ranch?

While the gap between the congregation averaging under 450 at worship and the one averaging 600 may not appear to be large, there is a definite break between the two. In several denominational families, a graph plotting the size of congregations by membership and also by worship attendance reveals a pattern of discontinuity when worship attendance reaches 400 to 450. A disproportionately large number of congregations cluster in the under 450 bracket in worship when compared to the distribution according to membership. A similar pattern is revealed in the growth pattern of hundreds of congregations. As they grow the membership curve continues to climb, but frequently the average attendance at worship begins to plateau. There appears to be an invisible barrier that keeps many congregations from increasing their average attendance beyond 400 to 450, even though their membership may continue to grow.

This break in the continuity of the growth pattern suggests that the congregation averaging 600 at worship is substantially different from the church averaging 400. Field studies substantiate this. It may be that one reason so many congregations level off in worship attendance at 400 to 450, rather than continuing to grow, is that to go beyond that point in size requires a substantial change in role, in self-expectations, in staffing and in internal governance. When these changes do not take place, it appears that the congregation has collided with a barrier. (As will be pointed out in the third chapter, it often is easier for legalistic or ideological churches to move from one size category to another than it is for behavioral parishes.)

This discontinuity is represented by a sharp change in analogies—from the mansion, where the focal point is concentrated in one place, to the ranch, which is marked by diversity and by many activities occurring concurrently in several different places.

Fewer than 3 percent of all the Protestant congregations in the United States and Canada fit into this bracket, but they include more than a fifth of all the Protestant worshipers on the typical Sabbath.

Just as a typical ranch includes a variety of activities in many different fields and buildings, lots of different creatures and a garden, the healthy huge congregation has an extensive program. The small face-to-face groups reflect many of the characteristics of the cat. The larger groups, such as the chancel choir of seventy-five voices or that big adult Sunday school class that averages more than seventy in attendance or the general meetings of the women's organization held every month resemble the collie. That is the place where a stranger often finds a warm welcome and is made to feel at home.

A Foreman...

**...understands...
that a <u>ranch</u> stands
or falls on its hands!**

— FRIAR TUCK.

Various organizations, such as the Sunday school, the men's fellowship, the women's organization, the music program, and the youth group, display several of the characteristics of a garden. They are the places where many newcomers feel needed and where they may gain that initial sense of belonging. Most gardens benefit from the contributions of additional volunteers. The two or three worship services on Sunday morning resemble a house and no two are exactly alike and they vary in size. Some of the lay leaders see the new house that was constructed recently for use on Saturday evening or Thursday evening as not worth the cost. After all, we can accommodate everyone in the two (or three) old houses, so why build a new one for such a small number of people?

Many of the people do not comprehend they are a part of a large complex ranching operation. When asked what they are doing, one responds, "I'm feeding my favorite cat." Another replies, "I'm helping with our smallest garden, but it's growing." A third says, "I'm taking care of the collie." A fourth declares, "We're remodeling the house in order to make it more accessible to the handicapped." A fifth explains, "I'm new here and I don't know what the others are doing, but I've been asked to help take care of this garden and I'm enjoying it. In fact, the main reason I'm here is because I enjoy working in the garden."

From a ministerial point of view, a fundamental factor in being able to be an effective senior pastor is to understand that, "While sometimes I feel like a zoo keeper, I know this is a ranch and I'm a rancher. I'm not a gardener. I'm not a housekeeper. I'm not a veterinarian who specializes in the care of small animals. I'm a rancher!"

One of the most important responsibilities of the senior minister is to help the members, and especially the lay leadership, realize this is a ranch and must be operated like a ranch. A big source of frustration for the senior minister is the large number of leaders, often including some staff members, who insist this is really a mansion or a house or a garden or a zoo and fail to see the larger picture. The primary responsibility of the rancher is to see that larger picture, to operate within a long time frame that is appropriate for a ranch and to resist the pressures (and often the temptation) to plunge in and "do it myself." The rancher spends less time "doing" and more time making sure the job gets done (by someone else) than does the gardener or housekeeper.

A common point of tension and conflict on the ranch is over the role of the laity. Some ranches depend on paid staff to do most of the work. Others project far greater expectations of the lay volunteers to feed the cats, nurture the collies, work in the gardens, care for the house and serve on administrative committees. The critical points of tensions are: (a) when the lay volunteers do not have a professional to turn to for advice on certain technical or professional issues, (b) no one thanks the volunteers, (c) someone thinks a part-time volunteer can take the place of the rancher or one of the full-time foremen, and (d) a few dedicated lay volunteers are able to mobilize a huge proportion of the available resources for use in one or two gardens while the rest of the ranch is allowed to run down.

Frequently the excessive expectations on the role of the laity run counter to the fact that it requires an investment of fifty to eighty hours a week to know about everything that is going on across the ranch. Few laypersons can make that investment every week. One result is that lay volunteers tend to specialize in one area (finances, real estate, Christian education, evangelism, or social action) which they can master with a reasonable investment of time and energy. Another result is that the staff tend to dominate policy-making for the ranch.

There are three routes in ministerial circles to becoming a rancher. One is to work on a ranch, be promoted to foreman, perhaps become the assistant rancher and then move to be a rancher somewhere else. The second is to spend several years taking care of a collie, spend some time as a gardener and/or a housekeeper before being "promoted" to rancher. An increasing number of lay leaders believe the first route makes sense. Most of the clergy, including those in charge of ministerial placement, prefer the second route.

A third route, which has been followed by scores of pastors in this century, is to find or plant a garden that has the potential for growth and turn it into a ranch. Sometimes this has meant relocating the garden to a new plot of land. This route usually requires a determined pastor who can see the potential for growth and involves a far longer than average pastorate. A favorable environment can accelerate the process, but that does not appear to be absolutely essential for the transformation. Scores of ministers in non-denominational or independent churches have followed this route and today serve as the chief honcho on a big ranch.

The Autonomous Nation

Approximately 1 percent of all the Protestant churches on this continent average more than 700 at worship on Sunday morning, but together the approximately 3,500 congregations in this category account for at least 7 percent of all the Protestant worshipers on the typical Sabbath. In our classification system these "super-churches" or "mini-denominations" resemble autonomous nations. (While the mansions, ranches, and nations account for 13 percent of all Protestant congregations, they include over one-half of all Protestant churchgoers and contribute nearly two-thirds of all the money that is given through congregational channels for missions.)

By definition a nation is an independent entity. It has its own distinctive history and its own culture, and it acts as an autonomous community with its own leaders. It also is convinced that it has the right to establish its own rules for the behavior of its citizens. It has its own unique procedures for selecting its leaders. While it may be a member of a federation of nations (OPEC, the United Nations, Organization of American States) most nations are deeply concerned that they maintain their own autonomy. Their autonomous role often is placed above their relationships with other nations in that federation.

The nation as an analogy for these exceptionally large congregations helps one understand why (a) such a large proportion of today's super-churches do not have any denominational ties, (b) a disproportionately large number of Presbyterian congregations leaving the denomination are in this size bracket (most of the independent nations in the world today once "belonged" to some other country—nations find it attractive to secede to gain independence), (c) it is not unusual for representatives from these congregations to be absent from meetings of the regional judicatory, but to be very influential in *national* meetings, (d) these congregations frequently ignore denominational channels in selecting the new senior minister and/or other program staff members, (e) several of these super-churches have developed their own curriculum series for adult Christian education (Bethel, Trinity) rather than turning to denominational resources, (f) these churches frequently design their own leadership training events and youth events rather than cooperating in denominational ventures, (g) many of these congregations own and operate their own camps or retreat centers rather than utilizing denominational facilities, (h) many of them sponsor their own foreign missionaries, and (i) most of them see and accept a responsibility for organizing new congregations (some even have used the term "colonize" in reference to starting new churches). Most of the churches in this size bracket bear a closer resemblance to denominations than they do to congregations.

An understanding of these distinctions also helps explain the differences in record-keeping among churches. To understand and administer the nation requires a complex set of records on members, programs, schedules, finances, personnel, and officers. Some specialists contend that to comprehend the nature of a cat, it is necessary to dissect and label each part. Most folks, however, know that the most effective way to identify the distinctive nature of a cat is to place a mouse in front of it.

A far more complex procedure is required, however, to comprehend the distinctive characteristics of a nation. The history of a nation often is written from an outline based on the succession of chief executive officers of that nation.

It also is relevant to note that nations sometimes experience a revolution as a new generation of leaders snatch power from an older generation that is reluctant to give up control of that nation's destiny.

Every year thousands of leaders from other nations, some very large, some very small and most of a moderate size, come to the United States or Canada to study what is being done here. Likewise the nation church often fulfills a very significant role as a teaching church and may even offer formal seminars or host workshops for visitors. It is critical to understand, however, that one gardener can learn more by visiting another garden than the leader of a nation can learn by visiting another nation. Gardens have many similarities. Nations tend to be unique.

The nation's president is in charge of foreign affairs, but usually delegates most of that responsibility. Likewise the senior minister of the mini-denomination church often delegates to staff members most of the responsibility for attending denominational and ecumenical meetings.

Sometimes when members from a collie- or a garden-size congregation go on vacation, they visit one of these super-churches, just as tourists visit a foreign country. When they return home, they may exclaim, "It was an interesting place to visit, but I wouldn't want to live there." They conclude that the term "big church" is an oxymoron. *

The president of the nation often is vulnerable to criticism from the press—much of it unfair—and so is the senior pastor of the super-church.

The larger the nation, the greater the proportion of the people who "don't understand where all of that money goes or what all of those paid staff do all day."

While small churches can govern themselves on the principle of functioning as a participatory democracy, the nation-size church fluctuates between a representative democracy and a benign dictatorship, depending on one's perspective. There are frequent complaints, "This place really is run by a small self-perpetuating elite." These complaints may reflect reality. Just as the ranch is run by the rancher and staff, the nation often is governed by the civil service, not by Congress. The civil servant is always prepared to explain "why that won't work here" or "how we tried that once before and it didn't work." In the nation-size church, just as is true

---

*An oxymoron is a figure of speech which combines contradictory terms such as "cruel kindness" or "thunderous silence" or "airline food" or "military intelligence" or "family vacation" or "civil war" or "independent church" or "wise committee" or "an independent Presbyterian church."

in Washington, many interest groups are not concerned about having "our own representatives" on the official board. They know that often the most effective place to be represented is in the cabinet or in the civil service. In the garden it may be very important to have "our representative" on the church council or board or session. In the ranch-size church, however, it may be more important to "know that one of the staff members represents our concerns and our interests."

In his book, *The Governance of Britain*, former Prime Minister Sir Harold Wilson includes in his list of the essential characteristics of a successful prime minister a sense of history and a recognition of the value of plenty of sleep. The senior minister of the mini-denomination size congregation carries many of the responsibilities of a prime minister—and that burden can be eased by plenty of sleep, as well as by a sense of history.

Finally, the change of prime ministers in this type of church frequently means a substantial change in direction, in priorities and in the way that community is perceived and evaluated by outsiders. By contrast, most cats, and many collies, adjust quickly and easily to a change in ministers—as long as they continue to be fed regularly. Sometimes the departing owner of a cat or a collie or a house leaves behind a list of idiosyncrasies to help the successor. When the president dies or resigns, however, there is a far greater loss in the sense of continuity. Sometimes the successor will retain all of the cabinet members for several months as a gesture of continuity, but eventually, as Gerald Ford pointed out, every football coach has a right to gather his own staff.

Questions for the Self-Appraisal Group

1. What size category fits this congregation? Cat? Collie? Garden? House? Mansion? Ranch? Nation?

2. Does everyone agree that that is the appropriate category for them? If not, what are the implications of the disagreement? Frequently it is difficult or impossible for congregational leaders to agree on the role God is calling that church to fill unless they can agree on contemporary reality. Does this congregation *today* really resemble a garden? Or a collie? Or a house?

3. Are we in the same category we were in twenty years ago? If not, what are the implications of the change?

4. What does our size category say to the role of our pastor? The role of our lay leadership? The role of our committee? Our relationships with other churches? Our relationships with our denomination? A change in ministerial leadership?

5. What does our size category say to our future as we seek to understand what the Lord is calling this congregation to be in the days ahead?

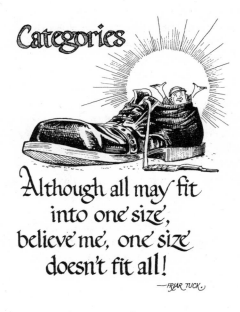

Categories

*Although all may fit
into one size,
believe me, one size
doesn't fit all!*

—FRIAR TUCK

2

IT'S NOT A BUSINESS!

"If I had a secretary as irresponsible as you have here, I'd fire her," Paul Rogers, founder and president of a manufacturing firm employing nearly one hundred people, said to the pastor at Central Church.

"This church has a $200,000 a year budget. That's a good-sized business!" declared Henry Crawford, one of the most influential leaders at First Church. "I believe the time has come to take a more businesslike approach to how we operate. As long as we're looking for a new senior minister, maybe we should try to find one who has a background in business."

"If I ran my business the way this parish is run, I'd be broke!" exclaimed John Andrews. "Sometimes I wonder how the churches are able to stay in business when most of them are so poorly managed."

These comments reflect the growing tendency to introduce business methods into the church, to evaluate the worshiping congregation from the perspective of a profit-making corporation and to manage religious organizations in a "businesslike" style. There is a grave risk that an *excessive* emphasis on utilizing business methods in the worshiping congregation can subvert the distinctive nature of the Christian church. There are deep and significant differences between a church and a business. When these differences are overlooked, it is tempting to become more businesslike—and that opens the door to subversion of purpose.

Three Types of Organizations

For discussion purposes it may be useful to think in terms of three different types of enterprises.[1] The profit-oriented company can be described as an entrepreneurial bureaucratic organization. By its nature the entrepreneurial bureaucracy demands, nurtures, and rewards a set of values, attitudes, and standards that are presumed to undergird that type of organizational structure and its goals. Examples of an entrepreneurial bureaucracy include the Ford Motor Company, General Electric, and Proctor and Gamble. (It should be noted that the term "bureaucracy" is used here in a descriptive, not a pejorative sense.)

A second organizational structure is that found in non-profit organizations and voluntary organizations. It requires a different, but slightly overlapping, set of values, attitudes, and standards to implement its goals and fulfill its reason for being. Examples of this type of organization include the YMCA, the Red Cross, the United States Army, the local public school, universities, the various service clubs, and the Girl Scouts. They all have a lot in common as we shall see in the next several pages.

The third type of organizational structure is the Christian church. Included in this category are worshiping congregations, regional judicatories, the national denominational agencies, ecumenical organizations, parachurch groups and theological seminaries. The last four, incidentally, are the furthest removed from the worshiping congregation, and they also are the religious organizations most often tempted to adopt managerial concepts originally designed for entrepreneurial bureaucracies. That may not be a coincidence.

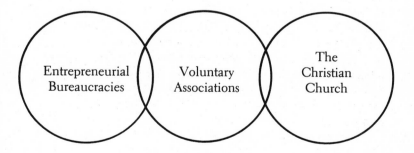

These three different types of organizational structures can be depicted by three overlapping circles with the non-profit structure or voluntary associations in the center. They have some unique characteristics, but they also offer a receptive organizational environment for some of the concepts and methods appropriate to the entrepreneurial bureaucracy and also for some of the attributes of the Christian church.

Another way of identifying the differences is to contrast the origins of these three types of enterprises. The Christian churches were created to advance a cause. Most non-profit organizations were created to advance a cause and/or offer a service. The origins of the entrepreneurial bureaucracy trace back to the desire to produce a product or a service and to make money.

If one prefers a personalized illustration of the epitome of the entrepreneurial bureaucracy, it could be Robert Strange McNamara. After serving as an officer in World War II, McNamara was one of the "Whiz Kids" who helped revitalize the Ford Motor Company. President John F. Kennedy asked McNamara to leave the presidency of Ford to become the secretary of defense. McNamara led the effort to institutionalize within the military a series of organizational practices and values that originated in entrepreneurial bureaucracies. He restructured the military to resemble the modern business corporation, perhaps without realizing that would result in a radical change in the ethical climate of the armed forces. The concept of management replaced the concept of leadership. Several scholars contend this led to the military disaster in Vietnam.

This same process has been underway in many religious organizations in Canada and the United States for the past two or three decades. In recent years it has spread from denominational agencies to parish life as both lay leaders and denominational officials encourage the application of corporate business practices to congregational and denominational affairs. The central thesis of this chapter is that by its very nature the worshiping congregation is most unlike an entrepreneurial bureaucracy and one should be extremely wary of suggestions to make the parish a more businesslike operation.

At the same time the churches have moved in the direction of being more businesslike in their practices and methods, hundreds of entrepreneurial bureaucracies have moved in the opposite direction by adopting some of the values and practices of Christian associations. These include the allocation of a fixed percentage of the net profits for philanthropic causes, granting paid furloughs to executives to work in charitable endeavors and adopting more humane personnel practices.

What Are the Differences?

There are at least a dozen differences between the typical entrepreneurial bureaucracy and the worshiping congregation that deserve our attention.

1. What is the bottom line?

The profit-making corporation has a single criterion for self-evaluation that is specific, widely agreed upon, relatively easy to measure, and simple to understand. How much money are we making? Are profits up or down? How does this quarter compare with the same quarter a year ago?

By contrast it is difficult to find a congregation—or a denominational agency—in which everyone agrees on a single standard for self-evaluation. What is happening to the spiritual development of our members? Have we shown an increase in baptisms? Are our dollar receipts up or down from last year? How strong is our evangelistic zeal? Are our people more devout than they were a year ago? Is our membership increasing or decreasing? What are we doing in mission and ministry beyond our own membership? How are we helping the poor and oppressed? What are the people in our Christian education classes learning? Is our Sunday school attendance increasing or decreasing?

Most churches usually find it difficult to agree on a single yardstick for self-evaluation and many of these criteria are subjective and difficult to measure.

This distinction has direct application when the churches become involved in goal setting, management-by-objective or similar business practices. This is not to suggest that the churches should not set goals! Most of them can and should. The difficulty arises when a business school approach is adopted, without modification, by the churches. Most goal-setting procedures or management-by-objective practices require (a) the formulation of specific, attainable and measurable goals, (b) widespread agreement on the priorities in the allocation of scarce resources, (c) measurable feedback on the progress toward the attainment of the goal, and (d) agreement on objective criteria for use in the subsequent evaluation. Most of what a Christian organization is about does not lend itself to these practices.[2]

While these requirements can be adapted to many aspects of church life, an excessive emphasis on business-oriented goal setting and management techniques tends to subvert the central purposes of the churches. The priorities tend to reflect the programs that can be fitted into an entrepreneurial goal-setting procedure based on a short time frame. One result may be an excessive emphasis on quantifiable goals such as a financial campaign, a building program, numerical growth, or the defining of the commitment to mission in dollar terms. "Every church should have a mortgage! Churches are at their best when they have a mortgage to pay off and the members can see the goal and measure the progress in moving toward it."

The translation of that cliche is that the managerial procedures adopted by any organization are not neutral decisions. The management procedures often influence the assignment of priorities and the selection of goals. When a church adopts, without modification, a management practice that is appropriate for an entrepreneurial bureaucracy, there is a grave risk that the central purpose of that church may be subverted.

2. Rational or traditional?

One of the basic differences between the entrepreneurial bureaucracy and the organization created to advance a cause can be identified by the doctrine of rationality. The profit-making business can and should be guided by a doctrine of economic rationality. A cost-benefit analysis is an appropriate managerial procedure.[3] By contrast the Christian church has a different basis for decision-making. Traditions, rituals, ceremonies, customs, schedules, and practices that do not make economic sense are very important in advancing the cause. These range from the decision to use the largest and most expensive room in the building only a couple of hours each week to the garb worn by the priest on a hot Sunday in August to the persistence of eleven o'clock Sunday morning as the hallowed hour for corporate worship to the huge denominational convention every May or June to a willingness to sacrifice one's life for the cause. The doctrine of economic rationality frequently is inappropriate for the organization created around a cause! The God whom Christians worship is known by faith, not by reason.

Another example of the distinctive character of the Christian church emerged in 1982 when the Presbyterian Church of Canada decided that ordained ministers no longer could refuse to participate in the ordination of women. Ministers are allowed complete freedom to believe what they want on this issue, but they do not have the right to abstain from participation in the ordination of women. Those who treasure a rational, logical, and consistent approach to decision-making may have difficulty with that action.

3. What is the source of tension?

One of the reasons it is difficult for voluntary associations, including the churches, to adopt procedures and practices that originated in the business world can be summarized in a pair of words—objective and subjective.

The well-administered entrepreneurial bureaucracy functions relatively smoothly when it can rely on objective-factual data in planning and decision-making. When a subjective factor, such as the intentions of the OPEC nations, is fed into the equation, the system flounders.

By their very nature most voluntary associations, and especially the churches, were designed to function with subjective content. Values, dreams, ideas, and personalities mark the organization created to advance a cause. These organizations were designed to accommodate subjective data. Ed Tucker has summarized this distinction, "The business world functions around nouns and verbs. The churches place a greater emphasis on adjectives and adverbs."

When subjective data begins to dominate the data flow in the rational entrepreneurial bureaucracy, the result usually is tension, discordance, and conflict.

When the organizational structure of the voluntary organization created to advance a cause is redesigned to be fueled largely by objective, rational, factual, and logical information, the result often is tension, discordance, and conflict. While churches can and should formulate goals, that process should be modified to accommodate the unique characteristics of the organization designed to advance a cause and to serve humankind. No one has been able to program the Holy Spirit or to budget the grace of God.

Examples of this discordance can be seen in the denominational efforts to use computer printouts in matching pastor and parish in ministerial placement, in many efforts at utilizing a business-oriented approach to goal setting and in allowing the budgeting process to become the central vehicle for planning.

4. What are the assumptions behind the personnel practices?

Historically the entrepreneurial bureaucracy has relied on two tools for motivating workers, the carrot and the stick. Traditionally these have been expressed through economic rewards, promotions, titles, demotions, suspensions, and dismissals. While the past three decades have brought some changes in the practices used to compel acceptable behavior in entrepreneurial bureaucracies, economic pressures still dominate the process.[4]

By contrast, personnel practices in voluntary associations including the Christian churches are cumbersome and slow, and economic factors are of minor importance (except in those denominational families that have modeled themselves after an entrepreneurial bureaucracy). The effort to compel acceptable behavior is far more dependent on the weight of tradition, peer group pressures, admonitions based on a commitment to the cause, seniority, tenure, loyalty to the organization, internalized norms, and the hope for a sudden change in the person's world view. Frequently no one individual possesses both the responsibility *and* the authority for changing behavior patterns. This is especially common in the voluntary association that is heavily dependent on the time and energy of volunteers.

In other words, the businessman who fires a secretary who will not meet acceptable standards lives in a different environment than the frustrated pastor who inherits a church secretary who was hired by a predecessor or a personnel committee and is married to the most influential layman in that congregation.

5. Self-interest or community interest?

Most profit-making enterprises depend on the pressures of self-interest to achieve their goals. These range from appealing to the self-interest of the consumer of the product or service being offered to the economic motivation of employees to dividends for the stockholders to bonuses for managers.

By contrast the enterprise created to further a cause typically places the interests of the total community above self-interest. This can be seen in the ethic of the best armies throughout human history, in the functioning of religious orders, in the traditional standards for ministerial placement, in the uniform salaries paid ministers in the Seventh-Day Adventist churches and in the dedication and the work load of millions of volunteers in tens of thousands of voluntary associations.

This distinction between self-interest and community interest is illustrated by the pastor who rejects the opportunity to move to a larger congregation with a higher salary, a more comfortable house, a full-time secretary, a fine office, and challenging opportunities because "I don't believe I have completed my ministry here."

6. What is the reward system?

Overlapping these last two distinctions is another basic difference between the entrepreneurial bureaucracy and the voluntary association. This is the reward system. In the profit-oriented business the reward system consists largely, but not entirely, of economic benefits. These include promotions, bonuses, perquisites such as use of a company-owned car, paid vacation time and sick leave, insurance and full reimbursement of expenses.

The typical voluntary association depends far more on "psychic rewards" for both paid staff members and for volunteers. These may include certificates, medals, citations, titles, the privilege of wearing a distinctive garb, a "pat on the back," applause, honorary degrees, inclusion of one's name on a letterhead, the naming of a building or park after the honored individual, and the opportunity to serve on a distinguished committee or as a delegate to a convention.

Even more significant are two more subtle differences in the reward systems. The first is that top echelon leaders in the entrepreneurial bureaucracy can and usually do expect a variety of perquisites that go with the office. These range from a private office to a company-owned automobile to employer-paid "vacation" trips to foreign tourist centers to first-class travel on the airlines to an excellent pension system to a personal secretary. Historically the "reward" for the top echelon leaders in Christianity has been sacrifice, suffering, death, and martyrdom.

In a different vein, the reward system in American business increasingly has been geared to a relatively short time frame. The year-end bonus is based on the level of profits over the past twelve months, not on a long-term evaluation. One of the major contemporary criticisms of American business practices is the excessive emphasis on short-term goals.

By contrast, the Christian churches traditionally have functioned on the basis of a very long time frame. As businesslike methods are introduced into the churches, there is a temptation to shift to a shorter time frame. Four examples of this are: (a) the increase in term calls in those denominations that have a tradition of lifetime or open-ended calls for clergy, (b) the decision in The United Methodist Church to limit the term of a bishop to eight years in any one episcopal area, (c) the trend toward enlisting Sunday school teachers and other volunteers for a three- or six-month term, and (d) the formal annual review or evaluation of the pastor's performance.

7. Leaders or managers?

The entrepreneurial bureaucracy seeks out and rewards managers who are able and willing to manage resources. The number one need in the churches is not for managers, but for leaders![5] Repeatedly Jesus expressed his contempt for those who emphasized the management of resources over the needs of people.

A managerial ethic tends to reward such institutional tendencies as (a) doing is more important than thinking or the end justifies the means, (b) loyalty means blind obedience to superiors without the freedom to criticize either the people at headquarters or the priorities that originate at headquarters, (c) an avoidance of any statement or action that might disrupt internal harmony or "rock the boat," and (d) an excessive tendency to place a high priority on one's own successful career.[6] Rewarding these behavior patterns may be appropriate in the entrepreneurial bureaucracy, but these behavior patterns are inappropriate for leaders in the Christian churches.

The churches need to remember the distinction made by Dandridge Malone, "Management is the 'physics' of things, but leadership is the 'chemistry' of people."[7]

The modern business corporation does need managers who can analyze data, weigh alternatives, recommend a specific course of action, and evaluate various marketing strategies. Business schools can educate people to fill managerial roles. The churches need leaders who can see the vision of a new tomorrow, inspire others with that vision, and by precept and example motivate those who share that vision.[8] Is it realistic to expect theological seminaries to teach leadership or to train managers?

8. Career or calling?

From a leadership perspective the most critical difference between the entrepreneurial bureaucracy and the Christian churches concerns the distinction between a career and a calling. The middle management employees of IBM may identify a career track for themselves. A move every few years frequently has been seen as a price tag for progress on that career track. (Some employees of IBM contend the initials stand for "I've been moved.") Such a move often was seen as compatible with the goals of both the company and the employee.

A Career or Calling?

"Only in a Calling does one do for nothing what others won't do for anything!"
—*FRIAR TUCK*

By contrast, for generations persons in several vocations have been perceived as engaged in a calling. Traditionally physicians, nurses, teachers, pastors, army officers and missionaries have been viewed as following a vocational calling. Serving humankind through a lifetime of commitment to a cause, not advancement of one's own career, has been a distinctive hallmark of the person engaged in a calling. Gradually, however, cultural forces have been at work to turn these vocations into careers. That transformation has been marked by a growing emphasis on credentials, by the emergence of career development centers, by evaluating the week in terms of the hours worked rather than by the amount of good that was accomplished, by responding to a proposed move in terms of the potential impact on one's career rather than the effect of that move on advancing the cause and by placing the needs of the organization above the cause which that organization was created to promote. Careerism tends to still the prophetic voices of the teacher, the preacher, the army officer, the physician, the missionary, and the nurse. Careerism encourages a change from service to self-interest. The rights, privileges, and perquisites of office become more important than duty, obligation, and service. Loyalty to one's superiors replaces loyalty to the cause. Image is seen as more important than performance.[9]

As will be pointed out later in this chapter, if it is assumed that ministers are pursuing a career, it is logical to adopt procedures for a periodic evaluation of their performance. If, however, it is assumed that ministers are engaged in a calling, the annual review procedures may turn out to be an effective means of transforming that call into a career.

9. What is the ethical code?

One of the more subtle distinctions between the entrepreneurial bureaucracy and most voluntary associations can be found in the ethical code.

The typical profit-based business does not expect the employees to subscribe to an overt ethical code. Such characteristics as honesty, punctuality, institutional loyalty, and "an honest day's work for a day's pay" are assumed.

Persons engaged in a calling are expected to comply with a higher code of ethics. This reflects a greater emphasis on values than on things or interests. Physicians, teachers, ministers, nurses, governmental officials, and army officers are expected to conform to a higher code of ethics, even when this runs counter to their individual self-interest. The pastor is expected to be willing to get out of bed at three o'clock in the morning to go to the hospital and the army officer is expected not to flee in the face of enemy fire, even though such actions are not in their own individual best interest.

10. Tradition or technology?

Most entrepreneurial bureaucracies find it relatively easy to accept and adopt technological improvements. The rapid growth of automatic data processing is a recent example of this trend that goes back to include the telephone, the internal combustion engine, the airplane, the development of a huge variety of plastics, and the silicon chip.

By contrast, organizations created to advance a cause often have greater difficulty utilizing technological advances. This point is illustrated by the old cliche, "Armies always prepare themselves to fight the last war." It also can be seen in the reluctance of most churches to use computers for data processing.

Perhaps the simplest way to illustrate this point is to ask the question, Which churches were the first to exploit television as a channel for communicating the gospel? The answer, naturally, is those congregations organized on an entrepreneurial bureaucratic model. Which religious organizations are most dependent on computers for record keeping? Which congregations were among the last to install a telephone in the meeting house?

11. Partners or adversaries?

Perhaps the most significant reason for examining the differences between entrepreneurial bureaucracies and organizations created to advance a cause can be seen in a pair of fundamental operating assumptions.

For generations Americans have assumed there is a built-in enmity between the individual worker and the organization in a profit-making enterprise. That adversarial relationship explains why labor unions are accepted as a necessary part of the American labor scene or why it is wise for the tenant to have a contract with the landlord. As major league baseball has changed from a sport to a business, the ballplayers have turned to agents to represent them and the contracts often run for several pages. Both major league football players and their counterparts in baseball now have unions to represent them in their negotiations with management. Strikes and the possibilities of strikes constitute news for the sports pages as well as for the business section of the daily newspaper.

While the Japanese have caused an increasing number of Americans to reconsider this concept, it is still widely assumed that adversarial relationships are a natural and healthy part of the business scene. (The federal Occupational Safety and Health Organization originally was organized on adversarial principles. Eventually government leaders began to recognize the health and safety of employees is a cause that is undermined by adversary relationships.)

By contrast, it is assumed here that the emergence of adversary relationships tends to undermine the role of the organization created to advance a cause. Not everyone in the churches, however, agrees[10] with this second assumption!

Illustrations of the negative impact of adversary relationships in the organization created to advance a cause include the Protestant Reformation, the strikes by university professors against the administration,[11] work stoppages by physicians to protest the policies of the administration of a hospital, the "fragging" of American army officers in Vietnam, and the withholding of benevolent funds by a congregation from denominational headquarters. Some will add to that list the emergence of adversary relationships in the Lutheran Church-Missouri Synod in the late 1960s, in The United Methodist Church in the late 1970s, and in the Southern Baptist Convention in the early 1980s.

When a minister views the congregation as an adversary or when the teacher is convinced the school administration is the enemy or when the hospital sees the patients as a nuisance and distraction or when denominational officers assume seminary professors are heretics or when the high school football coach believes his real opposition comes from among players on his own team or when the army officer places his or her own career above the welfare of the troops or when a congregation becomes convinced the real enemy is the bishop, these adversarial relationships will tend to undermine the health and vitality of that organization.

An administrative system rooted in economic values not only can tolerate adversarial relationships, it often thrives on them. That has been one of the prime assumptions behind the organizational structure of General Motors as Pontiac was seen as a competitor with Chevrolet, and Buick competed against all other divisions in that giant corporation. This emphasis on competition is a part of the capitalistic system. It also is one of the assumptions behind antitrust laws. By contrast, the institution created to advance a cause requires an administrative ideology that is rooted in communal values and reinforces community interdependence and obligations. A failure to understand these institutional distinctions has been a factor in causing many of the clergy to conclude socialism is superior to capitalism. As denominational organizations drift in the direction of becoming entrepreneurial bureaucracies, the predictable result will be an adversarial relationship between pastors and denominational leaders.

Adversarial relationships often produce craft unions. The sense of a partnership in advancing a common cause may produce professional associations, and when the merits of the cause are overwhelmed by the tendency to create an entrepreneurial bureaucracy, the professional associations often respond to that change by turning into labor unions. This pattern can be seen in education, medicine, professional sports, the American army, and the law. Will the clergy be next?

12. To be or to do?

The most profound difference between the profit-oriented business and the Christian church is in priorities. The first priority for an entrepreneurial bureaucracy is to do what it was organized to do. This also is one reason why, as the years go by, most voluntary associations begin to model themselves after an entrepreneurial bureaucracy. By contrast, the dominant imperative for the Christian church is to be. Out of that being comes the doing. The more the church drifts in the direction of the entrepreneurial bureaucracy, the greater the inclination to make doing the number one priority.

Why should congregational leaders engaged in a self-evaluation process be concerned about these distinctions between the Christian churches and profit-making businesses?

What Are the Criteria?

The primary reason for including this chapter in a book on congregational self-appraisal relates to the standards or criteria to be used in that evaluative process. Unless church leaders recognize this distinction it will be both tempting and easy to adopt criteria that are appropriate for an entrepreneurial bureaucracy in the evaluation of a religious organization. The criteria should be appropriate to the nature of the institution. Many of the criteria used for planning, decision-making, budgeting, and personnel practices in the business world turn out to be somewhere between inappropriate and counterproductive when practiced in the worshiping congregation.

Adopt or Adapt?

Second, while there are many business practices that have, can, and should be adapted for utilization in the churches, the key word is *adapt*, not adopt. Three examples can be used to illustrate that point.

Persuasive reasons can be offered why many congregations would be well advised to install a telephone in the meeting house. Unlike most businesses, however, the vast majority of churches should not be prepared to answer the telephone during the peak business hour.

Many secular budgeting procedures can be adapted for use in the churches, but most of these budgeting procedures have been designed to minimize expenditures. The basic goal in the churches is not to minimize expenditures, but to proclaim the gospel, sometimes in ways that do not conform to a cost-benefit analysis. Thus the congregation with room for two hundred worshipers, but only a hundred in attendance on the average Sunday, often can justify a Saturday evening or an early Sunday morning service, even though the attendance at that service may fluctuate between fifteen and thirty-five (Matthew 18:20).

Goal-setting processes developed in the business world often can be *adapted* to use in the churches, but (a) the churches do not have the freedom an entrepreneurial bureaucracy has to change its basic purpose or direction and (b) several ministries and programs of the churches do not lend themselves to traditional goal-setting procedures. The basic caution is that most goal-setting processes designed for an entrepreneurial bureaucracy will, when adopted by a religious organization, tend to encourage an emphasis on means-to-an-end issues and relegate to a secondary role the more subjective dimensions of ministry.

When bringing business practices into a religious organization the emphasis should be on adapting, not simply adopting.

The Evaluation of Pastors

A third reason for the inclusion of this chapter emerges from the growing pressures in recent years for regular or continuing formal evaluations of ministerial performance. While the pros and cons of that subject are too lengthy to be debated here, several observations are in order.

Most important of all, any evaluation of a person's performance must be based on criteria that are consistent with the organizational environment in which that person is functioning. The central thesis of this chapter is that the entrepreneurial bureaucracy is based on and also creates an administrative ideology that is substantially different from that of the Christian churches. Therefore evaluation procedures and criteria that are appropriate for an entrepreneurial bureaucracy may be somewhere between inappropriate and counterproductive when applied to parish pastors. Sometimes the criteria that are appropriate for one congregation will be inappropriate for another. One congregation may need and be happy with a pastor who emphasizes a transactional leadership role while another congregation needs a minister who is willing and able to accept the role of a transformational leader.

Furthermore, the employee in an entrepreneurial bureaucracy has a *job* or *position* and these businesses have accumulated tremendous resources for evaluating a person's performance in a job. By contrast, however, the pastor fills a *role* in an organization created to advance a cause. The accumulated wisdom and procedures for the evaluation of how a person fills a role in the advancement of a cause is very sparse. What are the criteria that should be used to evaluate St. Paul? Augustine? Martin Luther? John Wesley? Martin Luther King, Jr.?

Among the unresolved debates of contemporary society is agreement on the appropriate procedures and criteria for evaluating the performance of teachers, physicians, parents, judges, lawyers, husbands, wives, and presidents. Each one has a role, not a job.

An appropriate committee to evaluate the role of a pastor might include three mothers who are not employed outside the home and who have reared at least two teen-agers, a physician in family practice, a holder of an elective public executive office, such as mayor, governor, or council member, a classroom teacher, and the pastor from a church of a different denomination. Each one of these will understand the distinction between role and job.

Perhaps the most subtle point is that the typical evaluation process tends to nurture an adversarial relationship. A recent illustration of this can be seen in the process when a major league baseball player rejects management's salary offer and turns to arbitration. Both owners and players dislike the process because it naturally reinforces adversary relationships. Will the contemporary efforts to produce a formal evaluation of a pastor's role and performance nurture an adversarial relationship between the minister and the congregation? Or between the minister and the regional judicatory?

Finally, most procedures in use today for the evaluation of personnel originated with those who use a rational and logical approach to analyzing reality. That is appropriate for the evaluation of personnel in the entrepreneurial bureaucracy. By contrast, however, the Christian church is an ideological institution that does not *and should not* follow the rules of economic rationality. That means creation of a different procedure for use in a different context with a different set of criteria.

Many observers agree that the most important qualifications of the effective pastor in the small membership church, especially the collie-size congregation, is that she or he love the people.[12] How does one measure that? Likewise, as was pointed out in the previous chapter, the criteria for evaluating the performance of the gardener or the rancher will be different from those used for evaluating the performance of the minister caring for a cat or a house.

What Is the Strategy for Change?

A fourth reason for placing this chapter near the beginning of a book on congregational self-appraisal traces back to the question, how does one get an organization or institution to change its way of doing business in order to relate more effectively to a changing environment?

Three statements can be made in response to that question. First, most of what is known about initiating planned change from within an organization has been derived from organizations and institutions where the profit motive was the dominant motivating force. The changes in American agriculture were largely the result of economic forces. Second, comparatively little has been learned about how to initiate changes from within the organization created to advance a cause. The frustrations of agents of intentional change working from within the United States Army, the Roman Catholic Church, large urban school systems, and voluntary hospitals illustrate that generalization.[13] Third, most of the strategies that are effective for initiating change within the profit-oriented business are inappropriate and/or ineffective when applied to voluntary associations.

In summary, agents of intentional change who have been effective in an entrepreneurial bureaucracy may have to develop a new strategy and new tactics when they seek to effect changes in the organization created to advance a cause. Persuasion must replace economic pressures, patience must replace impetuosity, and collegiality must replace the hierarchical pyramid.

Where Are the Models?

A fifth reason for emphasizing this distinction between the business world and the religious community concerns the search for models. Where can church leaders turn, if not to the business community and the graduate schools of business administration, in their quest for wisdom, insights, and research that will speak to the management needs of the churches?

A simple rebuttal to that question could be stated, "That's the whole point of this chapter. The critical need in the churches is not for better managers, but for better leaders!" That, however, is a simplistic response to a complex question.

To illustrate the complexity of that question it may be useful to reflect briefly on five sources of models for the churches.

The best source from which church leaders could gain insights into the distinctive characteristics of religious organizations would be from research focused on the unique attributes of Christian institutions. Unfortunately there is a serious shortage of such research.[14] While a few studies have been completed, the type of critical research needed largely remains to be done. The big exception to that generalization is recent research on church growth.

A second alternative would be to turn to the research designed to analyze the characteristics of public institutions created to advance a cause, such as public education. There are two problems with this alternative. First, the published research, while available in huge quantities, is of uneven quality. Second, in most cases the reader has to translate the conceptual framework into ecclesiastical terms and interpret the application of the findings to the churches. Not everyone will be willing to make that effort, although the rewards do justify the time and energy required.[15]

A third, and a very provocative source, is the research on military organizations in general, and on the American armed forces in

particular. There are three big reasons why this merits investiga-
tion. First, in recent years a large quantity of excellent research has
been published, partly as a result of the financial resources
available for that type of research.[16] Second, it is relatively easy to
translate the findings of these studies into operational language for
the churches since both are concerned with advancing a cause.
Third, and most important, there are many institutional parallels
between military organizations and ecclesiastical institutions. The
parallels are referred to repeatedly in the Bible, in hymnody, and in
ecclesiastical structures (the Salvation Army is the most obvious
example). The most significant parallels can be found in the
current struggles in the American army and in the Christian
churches, both of which have been organized for centuries on an
hierarchical model, to respond to (a) the egalitarian forces that have
emerged since 1950, (b) the liberation movements including the
civil rights movement and the women's liberation movement,
(c) the demands to change from an authoritarian leadership model
to a more collegial process of decision-making, (d) the deterioration
of some of the traditional organizing principles that produced
cohesion and a sense of unity with new approaches to building unit
cohesion (for an expansion of this point see chapter 10), and (e) the
slowly growing recognition that the introduction of economic
administrative ideology and criteria subverts the basic nature of the
institution.

For those ministerial readers who are affronted by the suggestion
that the churches can learn from research about military
organizations, it may be useful to reflect on a few of the parallels
between the ordained clergy and the commissioned officer corps.
Historically both have occupied what the rest of society perceived
as a distinctive office, both have a custom of wearing special garb,
both place a great emphasis on titles and rank and the garb often
reflects title and rank. Both have relied on their own special
training schools to prepare candidates for that vocation and in both
cases entrance into the profession has been controlled by the
graduates, not by the general public. Until recently compulsory
chapel was a part of the daily routine in these training schools. Both
draw most of their administrators and teachers from those within
that vocation. Both have a tradition of a special commissioning or
ordination ceremony following graduation that includes the taking
of an oath or a vow by the candidate. Both are seen as "set apart"

vocations and the families of the practitioners are very conscious of this. Historically both have assumed that induction into that vocation was for a lifetime, or at least until retirement. (In both vocations the current generation of new entrants places less weight on that tradition than did previous generations. Increasingly both are becoming entry points into the secular labor force.) In both, the tradition has been that the needs of the cause, rather than the preferences of the individual, determined placement. In both vocations the practitioners, at an early age, had many firsthand encounters with death. In both vocations the handicap of a comparatively low salary was offset by perquisites of office, womb-like care from entrance to death, the mutual support of the brotherhood, the feeling that one was responding to a calling rather than simply "making a living," a sense of service to the public and a pension following retirement. (In both cases those now responsible for paying for pensions are beginning to show signs of rebellion.)

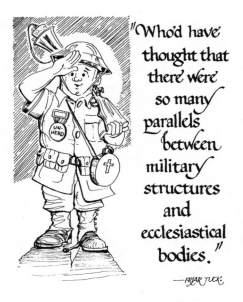

"Who'd have thought that there were so many parallels between military structures and ecclesiastical bodies."

—FRIAR TUCK.

In both professions the wife was expected to be the husband's helpmate, but celibacy was encouraged. Both have a long tradition of employer-owned housing, transfers at the convenience of the institution, special tax advantages, and an expectation that many practitioners will serve in foreign lands. Both vocations have a distinctive jargon, a tradition of in-house jokes, a code of ethics, a professional association, an assumption of peer group rather than outside evaluation, and special orders for the elite within the profession. Both place a great weight on graduate degrees and credentials in placement. Civilians have been expected to accord special deference to those in these vocations, but both have experienced a substantial erosion of these deference patterns in recent years. Both have a long history of an elite officer cadre who are presumed to possess certain mystic qualities. There are distinctive titles (bishop, general, admiral) for those at the top of the deference and command pyramid. The tradition that "rank has its privileges" is a part of the reward system for those at the top of the hierarchy. In both vocations there is a long tradition of the oldest son following in the father's footsteps. Both have a long tradition of naming buildings after distinguished members of that vocation. What is sometimes referred to as the "ecclesiastical escalator" has its counterpart in the military. Both have a long tradition that subordinates have an obligation of loyalty to senior officials that often must override personal inclinations. Both have been experiencing an erosion of the belief that if they are loyal to the system, the system will take care of them when they are too old to be contributing members.

Finally, both are vulnerable to the blight of "careerism," of placing the future career and well-being of the individual ahead of the cause.

If one is repelled by the idea of looking at public institutions or the military for models, the fourth most promising possibility is marketing. The basic thesis of the best thinkers in marketing is that an organization should focus on the needs of the people, rather than on pushing the organization's product. Leaders in the churches can learn from contemporary marketing specialists. [17]

The fifth best alternative in the search by church leaders for models is contemporary research and reflection in the business community, the social sciences, and especially the discipline sometimes referred to as industrial psychology. Much has been learned about the nature of institutions that can be translated into a conceptual framework useful to people in the churches. [18]

As you engage in the process of congregational self-appraisal, do you recognize that the church is not simply "another business"?

3

LEGALISTIC OR IDEOLOGICAL
OR BEHAVIORAL?

"Let's take a vote on it and let the majority decide," urged Sam Becker to the other members of Trinity Church attending the annual congregational meeting. "Our constitution states this type of issue should be settled at the annual meeting and the majority rules."

"When I first came into the pastoral ministry, I had to go to the Presbytery for permission to perform a marriage ceremony in which one or both of the parties had been divorced," recalled the Reverend Henry Elliott. "We had very strict rules on the remarriage of divorced persons in those days. I could conduct the wedding ceremony only if both the Presbytery and I had been convinced the divorced person was the innocent party in the termination of that marriage. That rule was changed several years ago, but for most of my ministry, I had to go to Presbytery to secure permission to marry someone who had been divorced."

"We have a rule here that all our Sunday school teachers use the King James translation of the Bible. To be more precise, we insist on the American Standard Version of 1901," declared the thirty-one-year-old pastor of the nine-year-old independent congregation on the north edge of the city. "We have nearly four hundred people in our Sunday school, nearly one-third of them are children and youth, and we don't want to confuse people about God's Word by using a lot of different translations and paraphrases. We stick to the one true version and everybody uses it. That way we don't have any misunderstandings over what the Lord is saying to us."

The Language of the Law

These three statements reflect one type of congregational life-style. These comments are representative of the legalistic church. In these congregations there is a heavy emphasis on rules, laws, decrees, and categorical standards. It is not uncommon, for example, to set a minimum age for membership on the governing board. If that minimum is twenty-five years, and a potential candidate will not reach his twenty-fifth birthday until a month after the annual meeting at which he would be elected, he simply is not eligible. In these congregations the minister is likely to use the word "law" as the contemporary equivalent for "Torah" (the oldest name for the Pentateuch), rather than the more appropriate word "story."[1] The language of the law dominates the conversation about congregational identity, role, and self-image. The language of the law also dominates the decision-making processes.

The legalistic churches have a long history of rigidity on the rules governing the role of women in the church, the requirements for the ordination of ministers, and the qualifications for church membership, including the removal of a person's name from the membership roll. These churches often take a very legalistic position on marriage after divorce (although this has changed in recent years as the pastor in hundreds of legalistic congregations has been divorced from his wife and remarried, or has remarried after the death of his first wife) or after the death of a spouse or the relationship of the wife to the husband and of the children to their parents. This strong legalistic orientation invites conflict (especially in the United States where the legal system of the culture is based on the concept of adversary relationships) and the choosing up of sides on issues. The stronger the legalistic orientation, the easier it is to transform minor questions into big and divisive issues. Legalistic churches appear to enjoy adversary relationships.

From a denominational perspective the United Presbyterian Church in the U.S.A., the Seventh-Day Adventists, the Church of Jesus Christ of Latter-Day Saints (Mormons), and the Christian Reformed Church in North America are examples of denominations that display strong legalistic tendencies. A substantial number of the independent or non-denominational churches founded since 1950 also fit into this bracket. Many of the churches founded as the result of a congregational "split" are legalistic churches. A substantial proportion of the congregations that "seceded" from the United Presbyterian Church or the Presbyterian Church in the United States are basically legalistic churches. (It should be noted that simply because the polity, traditions, and organizational structure of a denomination may produce a predominantly legalistic denomination that does not mean every congregation will be predominantly a legalistic church. Scores of United Presbyterian churches, for example, are predominantly behavioral congregations while even more are strongly ideological in orientation.)

The Language of Belief

A slightly overlapping category would be the ideological churches.[2] The distinctive characteristic of these congregations is the emphasis on the language of belief. People rely on biblical and theological words and concepts to convey the distinctive self-image and role of these congregations. Three examples can be used to illustrate that point.

"We liked the people, our two teen-agers really enjoyed the youth group, and we still have lots of friends there, but we simply weren't being fed spiritually," explained Susan Kellogg. She was sitting with her husband, Sam, in their living room and explaining to a visitor why they had left Central Church and subsequently joined Bethany Church.

"This is an independent church and I'm the second minister to serve here since it was organized in 1962. We're a Bible-believing, Bible-teaching congregation without any denominational ties," declared Ben Webster, the thirty-three-year-old minister at Calvary Temple. "We're a family church, we believe in and support the family. We favor prayer in the public school, and we oppose divorce, abortion, pornography, drugs, forced busing, the ordination of women as ministers, the ERA, and anything else that might undermine the sanctity of the home. There's a bunch of ministers in town who don't like us, but everybody knows exactly where Ben Webster and Calvary Temple stand on every issue."

"I guess you could call this an issue-centered church," reflected Mark Russell. "Back in the sixties our pastor went to Selma and marched in the civil rights movement. We were the first church in this community to push for a fair housing ordinance and we helped form the non-profit corporation that built that Section 202 apartment tower for the elderly over on Tenth Street. We consistently opposed the war in Vietnam and we housed a draft counseling center in the basement here at Faith Church for at least four or five years. This congregation has come out in favor of a woman's right to get an abortion if she feels she needs one and we've had a food pantry here for the needy for at least ten years."

"Yes, I believe you could describe this as a liberal congregation with a social conscience," added Terry Rogers. "I started coming here when I was in graduate school, and I continued after I graduated. I believe Faith Church lives up to its name by its actions. We're always on the frontline in social action issues. That's one reason, I guess, why we were the first denominational church in town to have a woman pastor."

Ideological congregations can be found all along the theological spectrum, but they tend to be clustered at either the theologically conservative end or at the theologically liberal pole.[3]

The ideological congregation often places a premium on a member's ability to articulate his or her religious beliefs and/or personal religious experiences. The typical ideological church often is built around a strong authority figure, the leaders usually expect a high degree of commitment from the members and tend to be intolerant of those who do not share the same doctrines, values, and beliefs.

The ideological churches are more likely than the behavioral congregations to take a strong public stand on such issues as abortion, inerrancy, homosexuality, the actions of the National Council of Churches or the World Council of Churches, the ordination of women, the theological stance of a seminary professor, or the separation of church and state.

Bethany and Faith churches and Calvary Temple appear to be examples of the ideological church. Faith is on the theological and social action left while Bethany and Calvary Temple are on the right, but in all three congregations leaders conceptualize the nature and mission of that congregation in ideological terms. Some observers would contend that Calvary Temple is representative of those congregations that straddle the line that divides the legalistic from the ideological type of church.

Despite the efforts to turn it into a legalistic church in the 1969-81 era, the Lutheran Church-Missouri Synod is an outstanding example of the ideological denomination. The Anglican Church of Canada, the Baptist General Convention, the

Fellowship of Grace Brethren Churches, and the Church of the Nazarene are other examples of ideological denominations. The Southern Baptist Convention is engaged in what promises to be at least a ten-year struggle to determine whether it will remain in the ideological category or shift over to become a legalistic body. The ideological denomination finds it very easy to elect a seminary professor as its chief executive officer while a legalistic denomination might elect a layman trained in the law as its chief executive officer or a pastor who represents a legalistic point of view.

The Language of Relationships

For those readers who do not feel comfortable with either the legalistic or the ideological type congregation, there is a third category. These can be called the behavioral churches. When asked to describe their church, the members of these congregations emphasize the love of the members for one another, the nurturing role of the pastor, the active caring by the members for anyone faced with a personal crisis, and the strong sense of fellowship. A member of one behavioral congregation explained, "In this congregation 'love' is a verb, not a noun." The leaders in these congregations place a greater value on how people live their faith than on a member's ability to articulate a particular doctrinal or legal position. Conversation in the behavioral church is dominated by the language of behavior. One study noted the remarkable "absence of God talk" in the behavioral church.[4] The pastor of the behavioral church tends to draw more heavily from the New Testament and less from the Old Testament in preaching. The behavioral church usually accepts and affirms that doubts and questions are part of a thoughtful and intelligent religious belief system. The legalistic church attempts to provide an answer for every question. The ideological church tends to see faith as the opposite of doubt.

In listening to members from the behavioral church describe their pilgrimage, one may hear stories such as this one that illustrates the distinctive personality of the behavioral church.

"You're asking me why I'm a member here even though we now live fourteen miles away! That's easy! There are two reasons. The pastor and the people," responded Betty Ferguson. She was sitting with her husband, Bill, in their living room and explaining to a visitor why they were so actively involved at Central Church. "My first husband and I were both raised in very strict homes and were members of a theologically conservative church when we were divorced. The divorce not only meant I had to find a place to live, but I also had to find a new church home. My daughter and I moved into an apartment building near the downtown office where I worked. That was eight years ago. About a year later one of my friends at work invited my daughter—she was about five at the time—and me to come to Central Church with her. We did, and we've been there ever since. It is the most accepting group of people you could find anywhere. Our pastor, who has been at Central nearly fifteen years now, is the most caring person you'll ever meet. He's been simply wonderful to us from the first day we walked in the building."

A Behavioral Bond

"We don't have to be alike to love each other!"

—FRIAR TUCK

"Let me expand on that a bit," added Bill Ferguson. "My first wife and I had been married about ten years when we moved here in 1972. We transferred our membership to Central Church and we both became active in it rather quickly. We didn't know it at the time, but my wife had cancer and died in August of 1976. I don't know how I could have survived the shock of that if it hadn't been for Pastor Don and the folks at Central. They rallied around me and the boys in a way that you wouldn't believe. Pastor Don was on vacation in Maine, but when he got the news, he immediately flew back here and stayed here with me and the boys right through the funeral."

At this point Bill got up and walked across the room, wiping his eyes as he continued the narrative.

"Betty and my first wife had served together on the Mission Committee a year or two after we moved here, and that was how I first got acquainted with Betty. To make a long story short, when Betty and I decided to get married, we wanted a simple little wedding on a Saturday afternoon here in the chapel with just her daughter, my two boys, and a few friends in attendance. When the word got out, however, it seemed everyone in the church wanted to come, so some friends persuaded us to move the wedding into the sanctuary. The place was packed! There must have been at least three hundred people there. After the wedding there was a reception and then a dinner in fellowship hall. We didn't do a thing to arrange it. The folks here at Central planned and took care of all the details. The wedding was at four o'clock that Saturday afternoon, but we couldn't get away from here to go on our honeymoon until close to nine o'clock that night. Does that explain why fourteen miles doesn't mean anything? It's never crossed our minds to change to a church out here where we now live."

The United Church of Christ and the United Church of Canada are two examples of denominations that would fit into the behavioral category. In several other denominations, including The United Methodist Church, the Episcopal Church, the Lutheran Church in America, and the Presbyterian Church in the United States, a serious debate is being carried on between those who believe the denomination belongs in the ideological category and those who believe it should continue to move in the direction of becoming a behavioral church. These discussions are being confused somewhat by a relatively small group in each denomination who insist that the denomination really should be more legalistic in its policy-making processes.

What Difference Does It Make?

There are several reasons why this threefold set of categories can be useful to the congregation engaged in self-appraisal.

First, this may be a useful addition to the categories traditionally used to classify churches. Instead of using denominational affiliation or size (large, middle-sized, small) or the theological spectrum (liberal or conservative) or the community context (urban, suburban, or rural) or similar categories, it may help to think of churches in legalistic or behavioral or ideological terms.

Second, and more important, this conceptual framework will help explain the increasing movement of churchgoers from one congregation to another. In the 1950s it could be assumed, and the facts supported the assumption, that churchgoers tended to follow denominational lines when they transferred their membership from one congregation to another. The dissatisfied Lutheran sought out a different Lutheran parish. The unhappy Methodist moved to another Methodist church. The discontented Presbyterian found another church from the Reformed tradition. During the past three decades denominational loyalty has decreased sharply. Today at least one-half of all churchgoers who change congregations, but do not change their place of residence, leave that denominational family when they switch their church membership.

Many of these changes can be described as from a behavioral congregation to an ideological congregation or from a legalistic congregation to a behavioral parish or from an ideological to a legalistic church. The highly legalistic churches have been unusually effective in reaching unchurched people who seek certainty and absolute answers to their religious questions.

This conceptual framework also may help leaders understand other behavior patterns. Shortly after her husband's death a widow transferred her membership from a behavioral congregation, where she and her husband had been members for nearly a decade, to an ideological church. Five years later when she needed volunteers to help her through some personal difficulties, she turned to the behavioral church for help. She explained, "I love the sermons in the church where I'm now a member, but I don't really know anyone there well enough to ask them for help."

The most important reason for including this concept in a book on congregational self-evaluation concerns the choice of the criteria to be used and the questions to be asked in the self-evaluation process. The member with a strong legalistic orientation will bring a different set of criteria to an evaluation of the youth program than will the member who represents a behavioral approach to congregational life.

Rules, Reasons or Relationships?

"Don't be left in the lurch, know what you want from your church!"
—FRYAR TUCK

This raises four fundamental questions for those responsible for the self-appraisal effort.

1. Is this predominantly a legalistic-type congregation? Or ideological? Or behavioral? While most denominations overlap two of these categories, each church tends to be predominantly in one of these three slots.

2. Are the leaders, including the minister, in this same category? This is a very important question. It is not unusual for the leaders to have a strong legalistic orientation when most of the members fit into the ideological orientation and a few belong to the behavioral bracket. Likewise it is not unusual to find the leaders coming largely from a behavioral perspective when most of the members are oriented toward an ideological and/or legalistic view

of the church. When these differences do exist that may be a source of divisive internal conflict that can be extremely difficult to resolve.

3. What will be the orientation of the members of the self-evaluation committee? Will the highest priority be given to selecting members for that committee who share with one another the same orientation, thus facilitating agreement on criteria and questions? Or will the highest priority be given to having the committee represent all the different viewpoints and values included in this congregation, even though this may create conflict in agreeing on criteria and formulating the evaluation questions? Or will the highest priority be given to selecting members for this committee who share the same orientation as the minister?

4. Will the criteria to be used in all phases of self-evaluation, from the women's organization to worship to church finances, be based on the same understanding of the nature of the church? Or will legalistic criteria be used to evaluate church finances, ideological criteria for evaluation of the youth program and behavioral criteria for reviewing the adult Sunday school classes?

Legalistic, Ideological or Behavioral

"What we see is what we'll be!"

—FRIAR TUCK

The greater the degree of agreement on these questions, the less tension and conflict that will result from a self-evaluation effort. The greater the disagreement, the more likely a self-appraisal process will turn out to be a divisive force.

Overlapping this last consideration is a very logical factor. Ideological congregations have a clearer sense of why they exist, of their purpose and role, of their strengths and of their own identity. This naturally means it is easier for them to choose a direction they want to go, to formulate goals and to implement those goals. By contrast, the largely non-ideological behavioral parish often has difficulty planning for the next chapter in its history. A church, like a president or a governor, without any ideology at all inevitably will begin to drift in an aimless manner. One example of the importance of ideology in planning is that those denominations with the strongest ideological orientation also tend to be the denominations with the most impressive records in new church development. One example of that was the Methodist Episcopal Church in the 1850–1920 era. Another is the Wisconsin Evangelical Lutheran Synod in the post-1960 era.

A fifth reason for introducing this concept early is the light it sheds on the oft-repeated statement from the Church Growth Movement that growing churches tend to attract new members who closely resemble the other members. This "homogeneous unit principle" is the most controversial statement in contemporary evangelistic efforts. Literalists have assumed this means pluralistic congregations cannot experience numerical growth—and that often appears to reflect reality.

There are, however, two major exceptions to the homogeneous unit principle. First, many highly pluralistic congregations do experience numerical growth *if* a sensitive, systematic, and continuing effort is made to manage congregational life to accommodate and affirm pluralism. Second, highly pluralistic congregations that fit the behavioral model often experience numerical growth. Frequently the only characteristic the members of the behavioral church share in common is an appreciation for that nurturing style of congregational life. The members often differ greatly in age, race, income, education, occupation, theological stance, persuasions on liturgy, social class, denominational background, taste in music and biblical interpretation, but they place a high value on nurture.

In other words, the homogeneous unit principle of church growth does apply to legalistic and ideological congregations, but has more limited relevance to the growth potential of the congregation that is predominantly a behavioral church.

A widespread illustration of this point is the Charismatic Renewal Movement. The presence of self-identified charismatic Christians in the behavioral congregation rarely turns out to be divisive. There are hundreds of examples, however, in which the charismatic movement has been divisive in an ideological or legalistic church.

A sixth reason why this is a useful dichotomy is in the selection of the next pastor. Frequently it is disruptive when the highly legalistic or ideological minister replaces the nurturing pastor who has facilitated the growth of a behavioral congregation. Usually it is less disruptive for the nurturing pastor to replace the ideological or legalistic minister, however, and sometimes many of the members are elated by that change, especially in small membership churches. The collie wants a lover more than a lecturer on what collies should believe. The least disruption from a pastoral change tends to be when the legalistic minister is followed by another legalistic pastor or when the ideological pastor is succeeded by another ideological pastor. Usually, because of the importance of the interpersonal relationships built up over time, it is more disruptive when the behavioral pastor is replaced by another behavioral minister. Relationships cannot be rebuilt overnight.

Seventh, while there are many exceptions to this generalization, long-established congregations tend to drift into the behavioral model *if* they have had the benefit of two or three decades of pastoral leadership that emphasized nurture and in which the pastor modeled the nurturing role. By contrast, ideological churches are found in disproportionately large numbers among (a) newer congregations, (b) long-established churches in which most of today's members joined since the arrival of the present minister, and (c) those churches belonging to the denominational families that have a very strong ideological orientation that is reinforced by the expectation that all the pastors will be graduates of the seminaries related to that denomination. The larger the proportion of the clergy who graduated from theological seminaries *not* related to that denomination, the more difficult it is for a denomination to remain in either the ideological or legalistic compartment. This is usually recognized by those denominational leaders who advocate a legalistic or ideological doctrine of the church. That also partially explains why the control of the theological seminaries is such an important issue for some people in the Lutheran Church-Missouri Synod, the Southern Baptist Convention, and the Christian Reformed Church. The weaker the denominational control over the theological seminaries and/or the larger the proportion of the clergy who go to seminaries outside the denominational family, the more difficult it will be to maintain a legalistic or an ideological posture for that denomination.

Many theological seminaries are subjected to pressure from the legalists to take a stricter and more legalistic stance in their teachings. Likewise the ideologists pressure the seminaries for a greater purity of doctrine in their teaching. By contrast, the behaviorists tend not to worry about the legalistic stance or the doctrinal purity of the theological seminaries. Their complaint more likely will be, "The graduates don't know how to relate to their parishioners."

The seminaries would like to be loved, or at least respected, by all, but most will settle for being left alone.

An eighth reason for lifting up this threefold set of categories is for congregations or denominations contemplating merger. It is relatively easy for two congregations or two denominations from the same category to unite. It is far more difficult and disruptive to negotiate and consummate a merger of two religious bodies that represent two different categories. It would be very difficult, for example, for the United Presbyterian Church and the United Church of Christ to unite, even though both are widely perceived to be "liberal" denominations. This conceptual framework also can help Lutherans understand why the Lutheran Church-Missouri Synod or the Wisconsin Evangelical Lutheran Synod or the Church of the Lutheran Confession are not eagerly seeking union with the Lutheran Church in America.

Finally, this conceptual framework can be used to identify the causes of disagreement and conflict over goals. The ideologists in your congregations may be convinced that Bible study should be the central focus of the high school youth group. The behaviorists may hope that the youth will learn to love one another and to discover how to act out their concern for one another. The legalists may believe the youth should be taught and learn what a Christian does and does not do.

In general, the more widely the membership is scattered among these three categories, the more difficult it will be to secure agreement on specific goals and priorities in ministry. Frequently these congregations display a remarkable degree of unity on a means-to-an-end goal, such as restoring the meeting place after a fire or paying off a mortgage, but become seriously divided when setting priorities for ministry.

Questions for the Self-Appraisal Committee

1. Is this predominantly a legalistic congregation today? Or ideological? Or behavioral? Do you all agree?

2. Is that the same answer that would have been given twenty years ago? If not, what produced the change? What are the implications of that change?

3. Does the current pastor have the same basic orientation as today's members?

4. Do all of you, as members of this committee, share the same perspective in terms of this threefold division? If not, what does that say to your assignment? What does it say to how you will respond to your assignment?

5. What will be the frame of reference that will dominate the selection of criteria and the formulations of the questions you will ask? Legalistic? Ideological? Behavioral?

4

HOW DO YOU READ
THE BIBLE?

"God created you and God loves you!" declared the pastor of the Maple Heights Church at the opening of the Sunday morning worship service. "Let us now join in singing 'This Is My Father's World' as we praise our Creator."

"Jesus is Lord!" exclaimed the preacher at First Church. "Our opening hymn is 'All Hail the Power of Jesus' Name.' Let us stand as we hail the power of the Lord."

"We're a spirit-filled church and let us express that as we join in singing one of the great hymns by Isaac Watts, 'Come, Holy Spirit, Heavenly Dove.' Let's sing like a spirit-filled people," urged the minister at Calvary Temple.

"The Bible tells us that God gave his only son to save the world," proclaimed the minister at Bethel Church. "Let us now join in singing 'O God of Light, Thy Word, a Lamp' as we prepare to hear God's holy word."

There are many different perspectives that can be used as leaders seek to understand the unique personality of the congregation of which they are a part and as they seek to discover the role God is calling that particular congregation to fill in his kingdom.

The system that is most widely used by "church shoppers" to classify congregations as they shop for a new church home consists of two categories—"friendly" and "unfriendly."[1]

Many clergy in classifying congregations often use a theological spectrum with "fundamentalist" at one end of it and "liberal" or "ultra-liberal" at the other end. In the first chapter of this book it was suggested that size can be a useful system for analyzing the differences among congregations. Another threefold system was described in the previous chapter. This chapter offers the

73

self-appraisal committee members another system as they reflect on the unique character and distinctive role of their congregation.

Why Ask?

Before exploring this fourfold classification system a word should be said to those who ask, "Why bother?"

Briefly there are four reasons for such a heavy emphasis on this aspect of the self-examination process. First, a useful planning model can be described by this diagram:

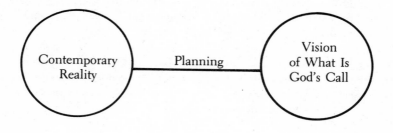

This planning model requires a vision of what God is calling that congregation to be and to be about in ministry. It also requires an understanding of the point of departure or contemporary reality.

A second reason for a self-analysis is the greater the degree of agreement on contemporary reality, the less diversionary conflict we will encounter on the path we need to follow to turn that vision of tomorrow into reality.

Third, the clearer our self-image, the easier it is for us to identify our distinctive role in this community as contrasted with the other congregations meeting in nearby buildings. In some cases this also will help us understand why the proposal for a merger with a congregation meeting in a nearby building would not be a productive course of action.

Fourth, this fourfold classification system will help us understand why certain people choose our congregation in preference to other churches, why some newcomers pick a different congregation, and why a growing number of churchgoers decide to transfer their membership from one church to another as they progress along their own spiritual and personal journey. This system also can be useful for congregations seeking a new pastor as they look for a good match between congregation and minister.

A Fourfold System

This system suggests most Christian congregations fit into one of four overlapping categories and that the churches in each group display similar characteristics. In one group of congregations the *predominant* emphasis is on God the Creator.[2] In another group the central focus is on Jesus as Savior. In a third group the basic accent is on the third person of the Trinity, the Holy Spirit. Finally, there is a large group of churches that are Bible-centered and their distinctive emphasis is on a strict reading and interpretation of Scripture. The opening paragraphs of this chapter offered a brief glimpse of these four categories. To help you place your congregation in one of these categories, it will be necessary to look at each group in more detail.

The First-Person Church

In the first-person congregation the Bible often is read from a theocentric perspective that identifies God both as creator *and* redeemer. The New Testament references to "Israel" usually are interpreted as referring to all of God's creation. There is a repeated emphasis on trusting that God is at work in his world and that he is in control today.

The first person, or theocentric, church usually is marked by a strong sense of joy. Spontaneous applause may erupt during corporate worship. Members from the theocentric church watched the George Burns movie *Oh, God!* and found it to be both a hilarious experience and a religious film. Many members from second-person churches had difficulty understanding how Christians could identify it as a religious motion picture.

The first-person church tends to be inclusive and to reach and include people from a variety of theological positions. It offers and affirms choices for people. The staff and members find it easy to see

good in others. It employs a broad definition of who may fit under
the label "Christian." A common characteristic of many of the lay
leaders of the theocentric congregation is that church is one of
several demands on their time—their family, job, membership in
other voluntary associations, hobbies, taking care of the house,
vacations, and civic duties. Frequently it is a pastor-centered
church. Institutional or local traditions may carry relatively little
weight in the theocentric church while creativity usually is
rewarded. The minister may preach more from the Synoptic
Gospels, in which Jesus repeatedly points to God rather than to
himself, and less from the letters of Paul. The preacher often
employs a prophetic hermeneutic that stresses the freedom of God
and places afflicting the comfortable above comforting the
afflicted. More often than not, the preaching is directed at the
congregation as a group, rather than to the individual.

If pushed to give a simple answer to a complex question, the
members of the theocentric church would agree that the central
fact of human existence is that God does exist and He is the creator
of all. There is a greater emphasis on creation than on judgment.
One result is the theocentric church often is perceived as a
welcoming haven by those who tend to feel rejected by most
Christian congregations.

In the strongest and most vigorous of the large first-person
congregations the members of the program staff often are very
different from one another in gifts, talents, interests, experiences,
and theological stance. This diversified staff is an operational
affirmation of pluralism. It also means nearly every member can
relate to someone on the staff as "my pastor." Occasionally, a large
and highly pluralistic first-person congregation will have an
associate minister who is the pastor to the second-person members,
a self-identified charismatic Christian staff member who "represents" the third-person members and another associate minister
who identifies with those members who believe the Bible is the key
foundation stone of the church.

The larger the theocentric congregation, the more likely there
will be an impressive variety of musical groups including vocal
choirs, handbell choirs, instrumental groups, and specialized
musical programming. The youth choir may be identified as "The
Creation Singers." Among the hymns sung most often will be
"Holy, Holy, Holy," "This Is My Father's World," "O God Our

Help in Ages Past," "A Mighty Fortress Is Our God," "For the Beauty of the Earth," or "All Things Bright and Beautiful."

The theocentric church often bears some resemblance to the behavioral congregation described in the previous chapter, but it is not a complete overlap. In the theocentric church, for example, the Christian concerns emphasis often is on social justice while in the behavioral church it may be on social welfare.

When the subject of stewardship comes up in the first-person church, the emphasis often is on *returning* to the Lord his tithe rather than on giving of one's own possessions.

Finally, in the first-person church one often hears more about life and less about death (although the age of the preacher often is the most influential single variable in determining this pattern). The theocentric church tends to lift up and celebrate the potential that God has given each of us, rather than to stress the limitations of mere mortals. The leaders in the theocentric church intuitively know the difference between desolation and defeat and they understand the perspective of the starthrower on the beaches of Costabel in Loren Eiseley's short story, *The Starthrower*.

The Second-Person Church

In the typical second-person congregation the central focus clearly is on Jesus Christ as Savior. The central emphasis is on salvation rather than on creation.

The preaching of the Word is central and music is seen as a supportive element to the preaching. The ministry of music usually does not have a distinctive identity of its own. The choir director often is seen as an assistant to the pastor, rather than as a program director. (This lack of clarity on the role of the choir director often is a product of an unarticulated but fundamental disagreement between the pastor and the choir director on the distinctive identity of that congregation. That disagreement, rather than a clash of personalities, may be the basic source of internal staff conflict.)

In the second-person church the youth choir is more likely to be called "Gospel Singers" or "The Salvation Singers" or "The Heavenly Heralds" rather than "The Creation Singers." In the Christocentric church the members frequently will display a strong preference for such hymns as "All Hail the Power of Jesus' Name,"

"The Old Rugged Cross," "Amazing Grace," "Rock of Ages," "What a Friend We Have in Jesus," "I Will Sing the Wondrous Story," "Fairest Lord Jesus," "How Sweet the Name of Jesus Sounds," or "Crown Him with Many Crowns."

When asked what they derive from the Sunday morning worship experience the members of the theocentric church are more likely to describe their response in such words as "joy" or "reassurance" or "uplift" while in the Christocentric congregations the members are more likely to use such words as "inspiration" or "comfort."

The leaders of the theocentric church often see the Christocentric parish as "conservative" or "fundamentalist" or "self-centered" or "exclusionary." The leaders of the Christocentric church often perceive the theocentric parish to be "worldly" or "liberal" or "social" or "not teaching the Bible." The members of the theocentric church often come from a very wide range on the theological spectrum while most of the members of the Christocentric church come from about the same point on that theological spectrum.

In the typical Christocentric church there often is a strong emphasis on the functional aspects of congregational life (education, missions, evangelism, finances) while in the theocentric parish the top priority usually is on the relationships of the members with one another. The theocentric parish often offers members far more choices for worship, education, confirmation, in the program of the women's organization and in the ministry of music than does the typical Christocentric church.

The pastor of the Christocentric parish frequently takes a very serious, sometimes even stern, approach to ministry while the pastor of the theocentric congregation tends to smile more frequently. The members of the theocentric church are more likely to express their feelings by spontaneous applause while the members of the Christocentric church are more likely to express their response through words. The theocentric church naturally will have a greater tolerance for diversity than will the Christocentric parish.

The second-person congregation often includes a disproportionately large number of widowed persons and mature adults. Some of them transferred their membership to that Christocentric parish because they wanted to hear more preaching on salvation.

The worship experience in the Christocentric parish usually is solemn, tends to follow the same format week after week and has a more passive role for the worshipers. (The two big exceptions to that generalization are (a) several relatively new and very large Anglo-Christocentric churches with an exceptional emphasis on music and (b) hundreds of large Black or Hispanic Christocentric churches.)

In the typical second-person church the emphasis on social action may be very modest, since personal salvation is the central focus. The operational expression of the second of Jesus' two great commandments often is on direct services to the needy and in some second-person churches this is a very large scale effort. The second-person church is more likely to be involved in partnership with parachurch organizations to alleviate human suffering than it is to be involved with neighboring congregations in the pursuit of social justice.

While it may not be stated this directly, in the second-person churches the dominant motivation behind giving often is guilt. The tension between the law and the gospel is a more commonly expressed theme in the Christocentric church than in any of the other three types in this classification system.

The redemptionist theme often is central in the pastoral counseling as well as in the preaching and there is a heavy emphasis on orthodox belief patterns. The preaching often draws heavily from the Epistles of Paul and the Gospel of John. When asked about the central question of all humankind, the leaders in the second-person church will be in quick agreement that it is on the need for each individual to accept Jesus Christ as personal Lord and Savior. Salvation by faith, of course, is a central theme in the second-person churches, but some of them place a greater emphasis on personal salvation while others lift up faith as the key word in that statement. In all discussions or sermons on salvation the emphasis almost invariably is on the *personal* salvation of the individual.

There is some resemblance between the ideological church described in the previous chapter and the Christocentric parish.

In the largest of the Christocentric churches the program staff tends to be drawn from among those persons who are at the same point on the theological spectrum, who carry the same value system, who are less concerned about offering people a range of choices and more concerned that the "right" choices are available, and who are more bound by tradition than those in the theocentric churches. In the second-person churches tradition may become a "choose up sides" issue over which is the correct expression of "our tradition."

In the theocentric church the discussions often focus on how to include more people while in the Christocentric church it is easy for the discussion to drift in the direction of deciding who will be excluded. (See Acts 15:6-21 for an early example of this type of debate.)

The conversion of the unsaved and the saving of souls are the central motivating forces in the Christocentric congregation for many programs ranging from door-to-door visitation to bus ministries to the financial support of world missions to new church development.

The Third-Person Church

While they are fewer in number, the easiest of these four categories of congregations to identify is the church that places the greatest emphasis on the third person of the Trinity.

The congregations that include large numbers of self-identified charismatic Christians are increasing in number and can be found in dozens of denominational families today. These churches tend to be marked by a high level of enthusiasm, a joyous attitude, and a sense of excitement. When compared to the churches in the other three categories identified here, the third-person congregations tend to display the least sense of denominational identity and tradition, to have the strongest congregational singing, to place the greatest emphasis on an experiential approach to religion, and to have the largest proportion of enthusiastic, committed, and hardworking lay volunteers.

One illustration of these differences can be found when the gathered congregation shares in intercessory prayer. Is the primary emphasis on concerns or on joys? In the typical first- and third-person churches the emphasis is likely to be on joys. In the typical second-person congregation intercessory prayer often emphasizes concerns and worries.

A persuasive case can be made to support the statement that the Charismatic Renewal Movement has turned out to be the strongest expression of ecumenicity during the last third of the twentieth century in the United States. One result is the third-person congregations in such mainline denominational families as Episcopal, United Presbyterian, Lutheran, United Methodist, American Baptist, and the Christian Church (Disciples of Christ) often attract new members who have had no previous relationship with that denomination and who do not bring a sense of denominational loyalty with them. It is not unusual to discover that one-fourth to one-third of the recent new members of a third-person Protestant congregation grew up in a Roman Catholic parish.

While there are many exceptions to this next generalization, the concept of the ministry of the laity is more likely to find a broad operational expression in the third-person churches than in any other type of congregation with the exception of the Quakers, the Amish, and a few other denominational families that do not have a place for salaried ministers.

Third-person churches tend to place a high value on witnessing to one's faith through music, and the hymns frequently exalt the Holy Spirit.

Their faith and their participation in church is more likely to dominate the life and weekly schedule of the members of the third-person congregation than is the pattern with either the theocentric or the Christocentric parishes. The motivation for giving in the third-person church often can be expressed in two words—thanksgiving and joy. Frequently a large proportion of the members of the Spirit-filled congregations not only tithe, but also give that entire tithe to the church. By contrast, the tithers in the theocentric parish often divide their tithes among several philanthropic causes.

If asked to identify the central facet of human existence, the members of the third-person church will quickly reply, "The baptism of the Holy Spirit," or "Letting the Holy Spirit take over my life," or "Being born again."

Finally, it should be noted that the third-person churches offer an excellent illustration of a universal shortcoming of any system that seeks to classify all of reality into groups. The world often does not appear to be the same from the perspective of those inside a particular group as it does to those who view that group from the outside. Many self-identified charismatic Christians will identify themselves as placing the primary emphasis on Jesus the Savior, a few will lift up above all others God the Creator, and others will insist their basic emphasis is on hearing, knowing, and obeying the Word. Most outsiders, however, will view the charismatic congregation as a third-person church.

Which Circle Is the Largest?

Many readers probably have experienced some difficulty with the first three categories in this fourfold classification system. A common response at this point is, "Now, wait a minute! Every orthodox Christian church is called to exalt all three persons of the Trinity! How can you suggest some lift up only one person of the Trinity? That's heresy."

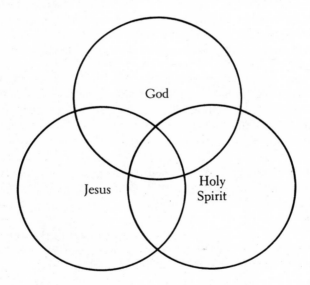

Without any intention of being facetious, the focus of this discussion is not on orthodoxy versus heresy. This discussion is intended to help congregational leaders identify the distinctive personality of their church. That is a different subject than heresy!

A traditional symbol to depict the Trinity consists of three over-lapping circles. The question being raised here can be summarized in such words as "predominant" or "central" or "basic." While your congregation may exalt all three persons in the Trinity, the question here is, Where is the *predominant* emphasis placed? On the Father? Or on the Son? Or on the Holy Spirit? Which circle is the largest in your congregation? Which circle receives the greatest emphasis in the preaching, in music, in education, in the discussions at committee meetings, and in the public prayers? (A simple and common illustration of this point is that rarely does one hear a prayer in a Christian gathering that equally exalts all three persons of the Trinity.) Which circle receives the greatest emphasis in the instruction classes and in pastoral care? Which circle do newcomers and visitors perceive as being dominant?

Some readers may reply, "All of them receive an equal emphasis here in our church." If that is an accurate representation of reality, that also is a very unusual congregation.

The Bible-Centered Church

Anyone acquainted with the contemporary church scene in Canada or the United States will have noted that these three categories do not cover the entire ecclesiastical landscape. Tens of thousands of congregations do not fit comfortably into this threefold classification scheme. The vast majority of the remaining congregations come under a fourth heading, the Bible-centered churches. Instead of emphasizing one of the three persons of the Trinity, the accent in these churches is on the Word. The Bible is the focal point of congregational life.

Among the common characteristics of the Bible-centered churches are the clear lines of authority, the emphasis on inerrancy, a relatively narrow definition of who qualifies as an orthodox Christian, and a tremendous emphasis on missions with a very high priority on the support of foreign missionaries. (A reasonable guess is that the financial support for 85 to 90 percent of all Canadians and Americans in the foreign mission field today comes from Bible-centered churches.)

The typical Bible-centered congregation also places a very high priority on education and the Bible is the textbook for nearly all of the organized study groups. The outsider sees indoctrination. The insider sees the study of the Word as the key to life and to personal salvation. In recent years the Book of Revelation has become a widely studied book in this type of congregation and today it may be the most popular book in the Bible in these churches.

The Bible-centered congregation usually stresses witnessing to one's faith through music, but that generalization does not apply to some of the very strict congregations in this category which forbid instrumental and/or vocal music. Gospel songs, rather than the Reformation hymns, dominate the selections for congregational singing in many Bible-centered congregations.

This emphasis on a correct interpretation of Scripture frequently means these churches will suffer from congregational divisions that may result in a split. These disputes over biblical interpretation often are expressed in struggles for power, including the calling of the next pastor, the selection of Sunday school teachers, the choice of denominational executives, and control over theological seminaries. Outsiders may be puzzled at the use of the term "liberal" to describe one of the factions in these congregational and intradenominational power struggles.

The congregations that fit into this fourth category also tend to be pastor-centered (except for those that do not have salaried ministers or those that have a long history of a large, well-organized, and strong system of adult Sunday school classes). The preaching frequently is based on an Old Testament lesson and often resembles a lecture more than a sermon. The members come in disproportionately large numbers from among those who are seeking reassurance, proof of God's existence, inspiration or direction. For many of the members life is built around family, home, job, and the church, and the whole family may be in church on two or three or four different occasions every week. In several respects the Bible-centered church resembles the legalistic type described in the previous chapter. The motivation for giving frequently has a strong legalistic dimension to it.

In several respects the Bible-centered churches appear to be at the opposite end of the spectrum from the theocentric congregations. The theocentric churches tend to interpret the biblical references to Israel to include all of God's creation, the second-person churches may interpret that as a reference to the church, and the Bible-centered churches often interpret the biblical references to Israel to mean today's nation of Israel. The theocentric congregations find it easy to see good in others and therefore tend to affirm churches from other denominational families while the Bible-centered churches place such a high priority on the correct interpretation of Scripture that they often find it impossible to accept new members by letter of transfer or to cooperate in any form of ministry with other churches. The theocentric Christian often sees the Bible-centered church as expressing a small or limited imagery of God's power or his activity in today's world. To some outsiders it may seem that the Bible-centered churches appear to feel a need to protect God, and those from Trinitarian churches have difficulty with the concept that God needs the protection of human beings. These conceptual differences are really more basic in the lack of cooperation between the theocentric churches and the Bible-centered churches than such hotly debated issues as "creation science" or "inerrancy" or the selection of an English language translation of the Bible. Trinitarian churches are more likely to take an inclusionary stance while the Bible-centered churches tend to operate from an exclusionary posture. That generalization can be seen in the differences of participation in joint worship experiences or the transfer of members by letter or recognition of the sacraments or cooperation in social welfare ministries or in strategies for new church development.

Perhaps the most traumatic experience for thousands of members of the Bible-centered churches in recent years has not been the issue of inerrancy or the debate over evolution or the proposal to ordain women. The most upsetting issue has been the divorce—and even more disturbing, the remarriage—of the greatly respected and highly visible pastor and/or lay leaders and/or the adult children of members in scores of very strict Bible-centered congregations. This has been an especially disruptive experience in those Bible-centered churches that are based on a conservative reading and strict obedience to the Scriptures.

What Does It All Mean?

This extended discussion may help one understand a half-dozen aspects of the contemporary religious scene.

First, as was pointed out earlier, while many congregations reflect the characteristics of two or three of these types, most congregations can be described as *predominantly* one type. Which of these four categories comes closest to describing the church of which you are a member? A useful exercise is to describe each of these categories, but without discussing which one fits your congregation. Before anyone attempts to place your church in one of these categories, ask each person in the group to write on a piece of paper the name of the category that appears to come closest to describing your congregation. Tabulate the results and let that be the beginning point for the discussion on defining the identity and role of your church. The greater the agreement on the corporate identity, the easier it is to plan.

Second, while this may not be the way the world should be, it appears that the numerically growing churches of today tend to come from among those that clearly, perhaps even over-whelmingly, fit into only one of these four categories. The "balanced churches" that display a mixture of all four characteristics tend not to be numerically growing congregations. Though that will distress some readers, it appears to reflect the impact of a clear congregational identity in attracting new members.

Third, the congregation in search of a new pastor may find this to be a useful conceptual framework in seeking a new minister. Serious, and sometimes highly disruptive "mismatches" occur when the theocentric minister tries to serve the Bible-centered congregation or when the second-person church calls a minister who would fit better in a third-person church. Denominational officials responsible for ministerial placement also may find this to be a useful frame of reference. (If it is true, as some observers claim, that denominational officials come in disproportionately large numbers from a theocentric perspective, that may be a partial explanation for some of the tension between congregational leaders and denominational headquarters. It also may help explain why occasionally the recommendation from a denominational official may result in a mismatch if that recommended pastor eventually comes to serve as the minister of that congregation.)

Fourth, this classification system may help leaders understand why some members have left to join another church. To assume they left because they did not like the pastor often is an oversimplified explanation. Frequently the ex-member has left a church that fits into one of these categories to join a church from a different category. (This classification system also may help explain why in thousands of families today the wife worships with one congregation and the husband is a member of a different church.)

Among the substantial contemporary migration patterns of church members are (a) from Roman Catholic to a theocentric Protestant church, (b) from a first-person to a second-person Protestant church, (c) from a Bible-centered church to a theocentric church, (d) from a second-person Protestant church to a third-person church, and (e) from a second-person parish to a Bible-centered congregation. Which migration patterns tend to stand out among those joining or leaving your congregation?

Fifth, for those interested in denominational mergers this conceptual framework can be useful. For example, instead of asking, "Why can't all of the Lutherans get together and form one denomination?" it might be more helpful to ask, "Is it reasonable to expect Bible-centered parishes to vote to unite with what they perceive as theocentric churches?"

Sixth, this classification system can be useful for those interested in intercongregational cooperation in ministry and programming. In general, cooperative ministries tend to be most effective, as well as easier to organize and maintain, if all of the participating congregations are predominantly from the same category.

This is especially important when two or more congregations agree to share a pastor. Too often that arrangement is worked out on the basis of the physical proximity of the meeting places of the cooperating congregations rather than on the corporate identity of each church. The minister who serves a theocentric church, a second-person congregation, and a Bible-centered church has a far more difficult task than the minister who is serving three second-person churches!

In reflecting on this classification system the rational person may be tempted to ask, "Shouldn't every church try for a more balanced presentation of the Christian message? Why should it be as one-sided as you suggest? Finally, are you suggesting that an unbalanced, perhaps even heretical, stance helps churches grow?"

One response could be, "What else would you expect in a sinful world?"

5

WHAT ARE THE WATERSHEDS?

It was a few minutes past eight o'clock on a Tuesday evening when the Pastoral Search Committee at West Side Church gathered for a special meeting. Their number one candidate was coming in for an interview the following Saturday afternoon. The members of the committee had been fully prepared to ask the candidate a series of questions. What they had not been prepared for was the list of questions the candidate had submitted to them.[1] At their last meeting, ten days earlier, the committee had run out of time before completing their preparations. The biggest item on the agenda for this special meeting was this question from the candidate, "As you look back over the last three decades in the history, ministry, and outreach of West Side Church, what are the events or dates or changes that stand out today as watersheds? Please identify for me what you consider to be the critical turning points in West Side's history."

"I've been thinking about that one ever since our last meeting," offered Harold Sanders, "and I'm convinced the number one turning point during the twenty-six years I've been a member came eleven years ago when we moved out of the fellowship hall for worship and into our new sanctuary. Our worship attendance would have stayed on a plateau if we had remained in the old building. Now it's a third higher than it was a dozen years ago."

"I thought about that one, too," reflected Dorothy Snead, "but I decided that didn't fit the question. I decided the question meant what has happened in the lives of the members and I think the second Lay Witness Mission we had here about seven years ago was the most significant turning point in our history. The lives of a lot of people were changed that weekend—and that's what church is all about!"

"You have an excellent point there, Dorothy," affirmed Ted Mason. "I agree we should focus on the turning points in our life together as a worshiping community, but I believe the key watershed was the creation of those small Bible study and prayer groups about sixteen years ago. If we hadn't created those groups, I doubt if we ever would have had the leadership to go ahead with either of those two Lay Witness weekends and I am abolutely sure those groups were the prime source of our determination to go ahead and build the new sanctuary."

"Who, what, when, and where' was your church turned-around?"

—FRIAR TUCK

"While it didn't involve many people, there were only eight of us who made the trip, I believe a big watershed came six years ago when this congregation sponsored a mission team to work in that children's hospital in Haiti," suggested Barbara Porter. "Up until that time we had only a nominal interest in missions and our Christian Action Committee was organized on paper, but it never met. Now we have a strong missions emphasis and our Christian action committee is one of the strongest groups in this church."

"I agree with every one of you, but you've missed the turning point that was behind everything you've mentioned," declared Andy Gustafson. "I've been a member here for thirty years, and the pivotal point in the history of this congregation was the arrival of Frank Evans as our minister twenty years ago this month. He was the sparkplug behind the formation of those Yokefellow groups.

He persuaded us to go ahead with the construction of a new
sanctuary when most of us were scared of inflation and what, at the
time, we thought were high interest rates. He suggested both of the
Lay Witness Missions. He challenged us to sponsor mission teams
to Haiti, Mexico, and Appalachia. When he left four years ago, he
left a big hole. In reflecting on all of what Frank did here, I'm a little
surprised his successor lasted as long as three years. That was a
tough act to follow! In all fairness I believe we should inform our
candidate that the sixteen-year pastorate of Frank Evans was the big
watershed here."

"We haven't heard from Sarah yet," noted one of the members.
"What do you see as the biggest turning point in our history here at
West Side?"

"I'm afraid I'm not the one to respond to that question," replied
Sarah Wade. "I've been a member here less than four years and I
really can't think of anything I could call a watershed or a turning
point during these four years."

This conversation illustrates another question that should be a
part of any congregational self-appraisal. As you reflect back over
the last decade or two or three in the life of your congregation, what
do people identify as the turning points or the critical forks in the
road that influenced the shape and priorities of today's
congregation? What has happened here that has had a profound
impact on the spiritual and personal growth of the members?

As you listen to the responses, you may want to utilize some of
these criteria in evaluating what you hear.

Evaluating the Responses

1. The first question to raise as you listen to the responses is to
identify the date. How many of these watershed events occurred at
least five years ago? At least a decade earlier? The central point is
what has happened lately? Are these watersheds ancient history? Or
do they reflect contemporary parish life? If one-half of today's
members joined during the past decade—and that is a common
characteristic among healthy churches—what proportion of
today's members share firsthand memories of those important
watersheds?

2. Were the principal watersheds short-term experiences that
peaked without a lasting impact?

3. Did most of the critical watersheds require a broad-based involvement of the membership? Or was the active participation confined to a small proportion of the members?

4. Were these watersheds built around a minister or a visiting celebrity with a passive role for most of the members? Or did they require the active and extended participation of a large number of members?

5. Who initiated that particular turning point? Is that person still here? If not, has that initiating role been filled by someone else?

6. What was done to build on that watershed? What was done subsequently to reinforce and perpetuate the "good things" that happened?

7. What members were most affected? How large was the group who was not affected? Which members apparently were *not* affected by any of these key events?

8. Were most of these turning points that people look back at and recall with positive feelings primarily member-oriented? Or basically outreach-oriented? If someone replies, "both," ask: "Was it *primarily* member-oriented or *primarily* oriented toward the needs of people beyond our own membership?"

9. Were most of these turning points related to (a) real estate considerations, (b) new ministries and programs, (c) changes in the lives and the faith development of individuals, or (d) the tenure and service of one particular minister?

10. If no one in your group or on your committee can identify any significant watersheds or turning points during the past decade, what does that mean?

After reflecting on the turning points in the life of this congregation, the self-appraisal committee may want to turn next and discuss some of the criteria that are used in the decision-making in their congregation.

6

What Are Our Criteria?

A couple of months after his arrival as the new pastor at First Church the Reverend Ed Gordon visited in the home of a long-time member.

"If you really want to make me happy, you'll urge the Board to go back to one service on Sunday morning," the member declared. "Up until a few years ago we always had just the one service on Sunday morning. Now that we have two services I don't see some of my old friends who go to the first service. I'm dependent on some friends for a ride to church and they prefer to go to the eleven o'clock service, but most of my old friends go at eight-thirty. I hope you'll be able to change it back to the way it used to be."

Later that afternoon Mr. Gordon stopped in to see a young couple who had united with First Church about a year before the new minister's arrival. As they talked, the husband commented, "One of the things that attracted us to First Church was that early service. With this schedule we go to worship early, stay for our Sunday school class and we're on our way by eleven o'clock. This is especially important to us because my mother, who lives a hundred and forty miles from here, is ill and her illness appears to be terminal. If we leave right after Sunday school, we can be at her home by two o'clock, have a late lunch with her and be back home by eight or nine o'clock in the evening. I have to leave the house to go to work a little after six on Monday morning, so this schedule suits us just fine. We try to get up to see her once every two or three weeks."

That same evening at the Board the issue of two worship experiences on Sunday morning versus only one came up again.

"It's a matter of simple arithmetic," explained one member of the Board. "We can seat two hundred, including the choir, if we fill every pew. Over the years our attendance has climbed gradually so now we're averaging 50 to 70 at the first service and 120 to 130 at the

second service. We have three choices. We can build. We can
continue with two services. Or we can try to pack everyone in at the
same hour."

"I like that third alternative," observed another member of the
Board. "There's something about a full church that makes the
worship service more meaningful. From the standpoint of our
personal convenience my wife and I would prefer to come to the
eight-thirty service. We're both early risers. We tried it a couple of
times, but it just didn't feel right. We missed the choir, the
congregational singing was weak and the place seemed as if it was
three-quarters empty, which it is when there are only fifty or sixty
people in the room. I believe there is enough room in back of the
rear pews and in the aisles for chairs on those Sundays when we
might need them. That way we could accommodate everyone at
one time. Maybe we should have two services on Palm Sunday,
Easter, and Christmas Eve, but the rest of the time we could find
room for everyone at the same hour."

"If you make that into a motion, I'll second it," came the
quick endorsement from another member of the Board who also
was in the chancel choir. "You're right about the congregational
singing. A full church sounds better than one that is half empty.
In addition there are at least five people who now go to the
eight-thirty service, including an excellent tenor, who would be
great additions to our choir. If we change to only one service on
Sunday morning, that will improve our choir. I might add that one
of the reasons the choir doesn't want to sing at the early service is
that we don't like to sit up there and look out over a bunch of empty
pews. It's bad enough at the late service in May when our
attendance begins to taper off and some Sundays half the pews are
empty."

"If we could change back to just the one service, that would
relieve some of the pressure on the schedule and the Sunday
school," added a representative from the Christian education
committee. "That could give us a full sixty minutes for the Sunday
school hour plus fifteen minutes for a coffee and social time
between the end of the Sunday school and the beginning of
worship. That also would give the choir a little more time. Now the
choir members have to leave their adult classes early in order to
robe and warm up."

Divisive Issues and Divisive Criteria

This debate could continue for at least another hour as various members explain their preferences on the Sunday morning schedule. The schedule for Sunday morning is one of several issues on which most members hold strong opinions. Others include the proportion of the annual expenditures that should be allocated for benevolences, any proposal to install a new pipe organ, the material to be studied by the children in the Sunday school, the choice of hymns on Sunday morning, the distance people will walk from where they park their car to reach the church building, the focus of the youth program and the size of the increase in the compensation of the minister for the coming year. The four most widely used criteria for making decisions on these matters are: (1) "This is what I believe," (2) "This is what I would prefer," (3) "This is how we used to do it here," and (4) "This is how we did it in the church where I used to be a member."

The issues mentioned here tend to be divisive questions in many congregations. These four widely used criteria for evaluating alternatives tend to reinforce that division of opinion. Rarely does everyone at the meeting share identical beliefs, preferences, recollections, and experiences. When these constitute the basic criteria for appraisal or decision-making, the result often is unnecessary and disruptive divisions.

What Are the Alternatives?

There are at least four widely used responses to these disagreements over criteria. One that is less common than formerly is, "Let the pastor decide. After all, we pay a professionally trained minister to lead us, so let's accept and follow that leadership."

A second is to delegate the responsibility to the deacons or the appropriate committee or the church council or the Board. Frequently all this does is to narrow the debate over criteria from the congregation as a whole to a smaller group.

A third approach is, "Let the majority rule. We'll poll those present on Sunday morning and discover what the majority prefers." This has some obvious limitations and some not so obvious. First, those present usually will tend to vote for the status quo, not for change. Second, what happens if the vote is eighty-five in favor of one alternative, and sixty-three in support of the other alternative, but a hundred and sixty members are absent? Does that mean those absent are disenfranchised? Third, assume the vote is on a proposal to add a Saturday evening worship experience. Will those who work on Sunday morning not be able to have a voice in this decision?

A variation of this approach is to refer all potentially divisive issues to a congregational meeting for decision. This may mean that the group that is able to rally their supporters will carry the day and leave behind a disillusioned majority of the membership.

A fourth alternative approach, and the one recommended here, is to postpone discussion on the content of the issue itself until after two prior issues have been resolved. That can relieve some of the divisiveness of the debate and make it easier to reach a consensus.

Two Prior Questions

The first of these two prior questions is, What are we trying to do? What is our basic purpose? Why do we exist as a church? What are our priorities?

When this question is raised in reference to the Sunday morning worship schedule, it can be stated very simply. Are we *primarily* interested in a schedule that will please most of our regular attenders *or* are we *primarily* concerned with increasing the number of people who come together for the corporate worship of God *and* our outreach to people beyond our own membership?

The distinction between those two priorities can be illustrated by turning back to the debate over one worship service or two on Sunday morning. List all of the most frequently heard arguments in favor of only one worship service on one sheet of paper. List all of the arguments in favor of offering people two worship experiences on Sunday morning on a second sheet. What is the basic difference between the two lists? In most churches the vast majority of the statements on the first sheet will be member-oriented reasons for scheduling only one service. Most of the statements on the second sheet will be outreach-oriented arguments that assume a responsibility to do more than take care of today's members.

Thus the first of these two prior questions can be summarized, Is our basic criterion in making decisions to take better care of our own members or to expand our outreach? There are times when that does become an either-or question. When that happens in your congregation, what is the outcome?

The second of these prior questions on criteria also can be stated in either-or terms. Do we spend a large share of our time, money, and other resources trying to do yesterday over again, only better, or do we concentrate our resources on the needs of people today and tomorrow? Are we more interested in keeping yesterday alive than we are in giving birth to a new tomorrow? Are we optimistic about the past and pessimistic about the future or do we believe that if God gives us a tomorrow, he will give us the resources necessary to be faithful and obedient in that new tomorrow? Are the best days in the life of this congregation ahead of us or behind us?

This point can be illustrated by three common planning questions in which the choice of criteria determine what will happen next.

Back in 1959 Zion Church completed the construction of an eight-room educational wing. Today the congregation is much older and only four of those rooms are used for church school classes. Another is a general purpose meeting room, a sixth has been made into an attractive parlor, and the other two are used for storage. One response to that situation is, "We need to buy a bus and bus in some kids so we can fill these rooms." A second is, "We should ask the trustees to build shelves and large storage cabinets in those two storage rooms so they wouldn't be such a mess." The third response is, "Would it be possible to knock out the wall between those rooms that are just used for storage and make one big room that could house a Mother's Club? There are a lot of young mothers around here and if we had a decent place for them to meet, we could start a weekly group for them."

The choice of criteria will decide which suggestion is approved.

The women's organization at Bethel Church includes four circles, down from nine back in 1971. All are study circles and one meets in the morning, two meet in the afternoon, and one meets in the evening. At a meeting of the executive committee someone pointed out that of the 384 adult women on the membership roll, only 82 were members of the women's organization and several of those rarely attended circle meetings. Someone suggested a letter to be sent to each of those other three hundred women inviting them to join one of the existing circles. Another suggestion was to ask the pastor if it would be possible for the four circle leaders to meet with each new member class and invite the women among those new members to join one of the four circles. A third suggestion was to start one new circle each year. One might be a sewing group, another a book circle, a third would be for women who wanted to participate in service projects such as calling on people in the county nursing home, a fourth would be a circle for mothers of teen-agers, a fifth might be a coed circle for young childless couples, a sixth possibility would be a circle for mothers of children in the weekday nursery school housed in that building, and another alternative would be a circle for single parents.

The choice of criteria will determine which suggestion is turned into an action plan.

At the September board meeting of the Walnut Street Church the treasurer announced that according to her calculations the congregation would end the year with a deficit of between $14,000 and $16,000. This announcement produced three immediate responses. The first was to suggest the name of a bank that probably would loan the church enough money to cover the deficit. The second was to ask the finance committee to schedule a special meeting to determine how much of the budgeted expenditures for the remainder of the year could be eliminated in order to reduce the prospective deficit. The third was a proposal to call a special meeting of the board to (a) determine how to raise an additional $15,000 before the end of the year and (b) decide when to schedule that effort.

The criteria that are a part of our planning and decision-making will determine which suggestion receives a favorable response.

Generic or Denominational?

One of the major developments in the food industry during the past several years has been the packaging and sale of grocery items in a plain package without a brand name. Hundreds of supermarkets now have one or two or three aisles devoted to low-priced groceries that do not bear a brand name and a large market has emerged for generic foods.

Another significant trend of the last half of the twentieth century has been the emergence of thousands of congregations in both Canada and the United States that do not carry a conspicuous denominational label. Most of these are independent or nondenominational churches. A modest fraction do have a denominational affiliation, but it is not given prominent visibility. This trend is far more visible in the western third of the continent than in the eastern third, but it appears to be a growing movement. One of the obvious motivating forces is the effort by a new church to reach people from a variety of denominational backgrounds. Another is the decline in denominational loyalty. A third is disenchantment with the actions of some national denominational agencies and the desire to minimize the denominational relationship. A fourth factor is the organization of thousands of new congregations by ministers who do not have a denominational affiliation. This is especially common with third-person churches (see chapter 4), with hundreds of congregations founded by a minister born, reared, and trained in Asia, Latin America, or Europe, with graduates of "transdenominational" seminaries and with a significant number of black ministers. A fifth reason for the recent increase in the number of independent congregations is in the basic nature of many Bible-centered churches. Many of them interpret the Bible in a manner that makes it impossible to identify themselves as a member of a denominational family. A sixth factor has been the confusion over name recognition for some of the denominations, such as the Reformed Church in America or the United Church of Christ that have been interested in starting new congregations in the South and Southwest. The mission developer pastor often concluded that the prominent display of terms, such as "Reformed Church" or "Church of Christ," was a liability rather than an asset. Finally there appears to be a widespread belief that a radio or television preacher can reach a larger audience—and receive financial support from more listeners—if that program does not carry a denominational label. Like generic groceries, these "generic churches" have attracted a large following in recent years.

Does your congregation see itself primarily as a denominationally related church or a community or nondenominational or transdenominational or independent church?

This is an extremely significant part of the self-image. It also becomes a very influential criterion in making hundreds of administrative and programmatic decisions ranging from the format for youth ministries to the allocation of financial resources for missions to the selection of curriculum materials in the educational program to the name on the meeting house to the administration of the sacraments to the definition of the church year to the title for congregational officers to the system for resolving internal disputes.

There are some people, including this writer, who believe that a careful reading of the New Testament eliminates the choice of being an independent church. The term "independent church" is a contradiction in terms and belongs in the same category with such other oxymorons. By definition Christian churches must share a sense of interdependence.

Is your congregation a generic church or does it carry and affirm a denominational affiliation?

Political or Performance?

"If we're going to have a long-range planning committee here, we need to be sure it's representative of our entire membership," urged Elmer Stauffer to the other leaders at Broad Street Church. The subject under consideration was a proposal from the new minister to create a special committee to study the future and to bring in specific action recommendations for expanding the outreach and program of this seventy-seven-year-old congregation. The congregation had enjoyed the twenty-three-year pastorate of Dr. John Harrison, a highly respected minister who had retired three years earlier. He was followed by a thirty-seven-year-old pastor who suddenly, after only twenty-two months at Broad Street, announced he was leaving the professional ministry for a career as a family counselor. The congregation had drifted during the last few years of Dr. Harrison's tenure and had continued to drift during the brief pastorage of the successor. A denominational official called it "a church in transition." Everyone agreed that "the good old days" were in the past, but there was no agreement on what the future might bring. This impasse produced the suggestion for creating a long-range planning committee.

"I agree with you, Elmer," declared another long-time member. "We need to be sure that every group, organization, faction, and committee is represented on this committee. We want to be sure that everyone's opinion is heard and that no one is ignored."

This conversation raises another very important issue that must be considered by any congregation or task force on the future. What will be the criteria that will be used to select members of that committee? Three alternatives merit consideration here.

The first is the most common. This is to select the membership so that every viewpoint, value system, group, organization, program, faction, clan, and segment of the congregation will be represented on the planning committee. This criterion has much to commend it in the selection of members to a *decision-making* body such as the church council or vestry or board or session, but it may not be the most desirable yardstick to use in selecting members for a long-range planning committee.

The representative approach to constituting such a committee usually means (a) creating a large and sometimes unwieldy committee, (b) including a disproportionately large number of long-time members, (c) selecting representatives from such administrative committees as finance, personnel, and trustees as well as from program areas such as education, worship, and evangelism, (d) creating barriers to agreement among the members on the need for major changes in direction and priorities, (e) risking an overemphasis on symptoms and on means-to-an-end concerns such as real estate or finances while basic questions on purpose and role are neglected, and (f) spending a substantial amount of committee time to work out compromises on opposing points of view.

A second approach is to emphasize the concept of participatory democracy. This has much to commend it in smaller congregations with fewer than eighty to one hundred members and in some religious bodies such as the Quakers. (Presbyterians, Lutherans, Episcopalians, and others who function in a system of church government based on representative democracy may want to skip the next paragraph since it does not apply to their polity.)

Leaders in larger congregations, however, should be aware that the recent history of participatory democracy has been marked by three patterns. First, participatory democracy means every group, except the next generation, has a veto. Since the only thing that cannot be vetoed is the status quo, participatory democracy has turned out to be an effective means of immobilizing an organization that must respond to a changing context. The United States Congress is a notable example. Second, the greater the emphasis on participatory democracy in planning and decision-making, the more likely that organization will repel the people it is seeking to reach and serve. Third, the larger the organization, the easier it is in a governance system based on participatory democracy for a few to frustrate the wishes of the majority.

A third alternative is to emphasize performance in the selection of the members of a long-range planning committee. If "doing a good job and getting that job done" becomes the basic criterion for selecting members of the task force on the future, consideration should be given to choosing a relatively homogeneous group who (a) share a common doctrine of the Christian church and a common theological belief system, (b) have a high level of agreement on what God is calling this congregation to be and to be about in the years ahead, (c) agree on the nature of contemporary reality (see the planning model described on page 74), (d) share a strong future orientation and display little interest in proposals to reinvent yesterday, (e) are supportive of the present pastor, (f) are willing to take the initiative and to lead, (g) place a high value on creativity, (h) understand the reality of trade offs in planning and decision-making, (i) are comfortable when dealing with abstract concepts, (j) possess above average skills in communication, (k) include at least one or two recent new members of this congregation, (l) share a strong Christian commitment to and understanding of the religious and institutional dimensions of the worshiping congregation, understand the reality of trade offs, and (m) do not feel a compulsion to meet and act in secret.

Ideally this committee will include no more than seven persons including the pastor.

How do these criteria match the ones used in your congregation in selecting the members for a long-range planning committee?

7

WHAT ARE OUR
MEMBERSHIP TRENDS?

After a self-appraisal committee has been formed, and after the members have reviewed their assignment and reflected on the questions raised in these first six chapters, the next appropriate step may be to review membership trends.

One obvious reason for this is to identify the characteristics that reflect size. Is this a collie-size congregation? Or a garden? Or a ranch?

In reviewing the size of the congregation three sets of statistics should be assembled for this phase of the self-appraisal. The first is a tabulation of the membership for each of the past ten to twelve years. What has been the trend? Up or down? Why?

More useful, but sometimes more difficult to gather, is the average attendance at worship for each of the past dozen years. If your church offers two or three services (perhaps one on Thursday or Saturday evening and two on Sunday morning), the combined figures should be used. Worship attendance is a more sensitive barometer of change and a better diagnostic tool than any other statistic. It also is the best indicator for measuring size, for estimating the work load for staff, for predicting the level of member giving, for comparing the resources of one congregation with another, and for evaluating the participation rate.

The third of these historical statistical accounts that should be gathered is the average attendance (not the enrollment) in the Sunday church school. If the data are available, three very useful subcategories are: (a) number of children on the nursery roll for each of the past several years, (b) the average attendance in the five-year-old class for each of the past several years, and (c) the average attendance in grades one to four combined for each of the past several years. These figures will give an indication as to whether your congregation is reaching the families responsible for the new baby boom that began in 1977.

103

These figures also will help your committee discover the impact of changes in size. The congregation that is double the size, or one-half the size it was ten years earlier probably also changed significantly in other respects.

In addition to these three sets of historical data on membership trends there are several additional questions that can and should be asked in the early stages of the self-appraisal process. The first of these may be the most revealing.

What Is Our Turnover Rate?

In varying degrees every congregation represents a passing parade of parishioners. The three-hundred-member congregation of today that also was a three-hundred-member church a dozen years ago is not the same church it was back then. The size appears to be the same, but only half of the people who were members a dozen years ago are still members today. Time means turnover and turnover brings change.

A useful tabulation is to measure this turnover on a year-by-year basis for the past decade.

The following table shows the turnover in a four-hundred-member congregation in a city of nearly 40,000 residents. All of the figures refer to the confirmed membership.

This is a typical four-hundred-confirmed-member congregation. Each year, on the average, approximately 7 percent of the members die, transfer their membership to other churches, or simply "drop out" and their names eventually are removed from the membership roster by action of the governing board. It also is typical in that (a) more than one-half of the losses come via the dropout route, (b) member deaths average approximately twelve per 1,000 members per year, (c) new members received via confirmation, adult baptisms, and profession of faith average approximately 32 per 1,000 confirmed members per year, (d) losses by the combined total of transfers and dropouts average 60 per 1,000 confirmed members per year. Those are representative figures for (a) middle-sized congregations, (b) congregations located in a city or urban community with an average turnover in the population, (c) those with an age distribution reflecting the national pattern (those congregations with an older membership tend to have a higher death rate, but a lower overall turnover rate), and (d) those that have remained on a plateau in size.

Membership Turnover

	Gains		Losses			
Year	Transfers In	Confirmations & Prof. of Faith	Deaths	Transfers Out	"Dropouts"*	Net
1975	16	12	5	6	12	5
1976	13	8	3	0	15	3
1977	19	14	9	11	10	3
1978	21	17	4	8	21	5
1979	8	9	6	14	11	−14
1980	33	6	3	3	15	18
1981	8	13	7	0	22	− 8
1982	10	15	2	19	17	−13
1983	13	16	8	12	8	1
1984	19	20	3	7	19	10
Avg.	16	13	5	8	15	1

*This column represents those persons who no longer are active members. Some have united with other churches without asking for a transfer of membership. Others have moved and left no word of their intentions. Several still live here, but have dropped out of an active role.

Larger congregations and/or growing churches tend to receive a larger number of new members annually while smaller congregations and numerically declining churches may have a smaller number of new members. The stable one-hundred-member congregation, for example, may lose one or two members by death in the average year, have one dropout, and lose two other members by transfer. By contrast, the thousand-member congregation, which typically has a much higher turnover rate, may lose a dozen to twenty members per year by death, thirty to fifty through transfers to other churches, and another forty to sixty who drop out.

(In many congregations the record-keeping procedures may make it difficult to determine the dropout rate. A common pattern is to "clean the rolls" once every eight or ten years. This may require you to estimate the dropout rate on a year-by-year basis, based on figures for a longer time frame. It may be useful to know that spot surveys indicate that one-fourth to one-third of the persons who have their name removed from the membership roll

by action of the governing board had already united with another
congregation by the time that action had been taken.)

Baptisms, Confirmations, and Deaths

Three other sets of trend lines that overlap the turnover rate also
merit review. The first is the number of baptisms. If your
congregation practices infant baptism, a keeping-up-with-the-
population rate would mean (a) you have been averaging 2.5 to 3.0
infant and child baptisms per hundred confirmed members (or 2.0
to 2.5 per hundred baptized members) per year and (b) that rate has
been going up in recent years. Thus the four-hundred-confirmed-
member congregation would average ten to twelve infant and child
baptisms per year if it included an average proportion of younger
families and perhaps fifteen to twenty per year if it was unusually
effective in reaching younger families. The rate for the early and
mid-eighties should be 15 to 30 percent higher than the rate for the
early and mid-seventies in response to the increase in the number
of births.

In the average Protestant congregation the number of new
members received by profession of faith or adult baptism or
confirmation (including youth who were confirmed) will be
approximately three per one hundred members per year. In
growing churches that often will be closer to four or five or six per
one hundred members, and in rapidly growing congregations it
may be as high as ten or twelve per one hundred members on an
annual basis. If it averages less than two per one hundred members
per year, that usually is a sign of a numerically declining church.

The death rate for the residents of Canada and the United States
averages approximately nine per thousand residents per year. For
those churches that report membership on the basis of the total
number of baptized persons that means a death rate of nine per
thousand members would be average. The death rate in the
mainline Protestant denominations is slightly more than twelve per
thousand confirmed members.

In many large downtown churches the death rate may be as
much as twenty-five to thirty-five per one thousand confirmed
members per year while in newer suburban congregations it may be
as low as one or two per thousand confirmed members per year and
rarely is above five per thousand.

What is the death *rate* in your congregation? Was the rate over the past five years higher or lower than the denominational average?

The Tenure of Today's Members

Finally, two questions should be asked about the tenure of today's members. These rank, along with the question mentioned earlier on the average attendance at worship, as the three most revealing statistical questions on membership trends.

First, what is the median tenure of today's confirmed members? One-half of today's members joined before a certain date and the other half joined since that date. What is that date? In the typical Protestant congregation that has been on a plateau in size that date will be between ten and twelve years ago. (In rural churches and in downtown churches it often is eleven to fourteen years ago. In suburban and smaller city churches it usually is nine to eleven years ago.) If that date is less than seven years ago (except, obviously, for new churches organized within the past decade) it suggests the congregation may be receiving new members at a faster pace than they can be assimilated. If that date is more than ten to twelve years ago, it often means an erosion of the ability of that congregation to reach, attract, and receive new members.

While it is far from a universal pattern, there also is a tendency in the congregations in which that date is less than ten years to be more open to change while those in which that date is more than fifteen years ago tend to be more resistant to innovation.

The second question on tenure is illustrated by the box on the next page, which shows the tenure of today's members in a 1,200 member downtown congregation in a city of 350,000 residents. Like many long established downtown churches (a) one-third of today's members were classified as inactive, (b) one-half had been members for sixteen years or longer and one-half for less than sixteen years, (c) the largest single group of today's inactives joined during the leadership of a pastor with a magnetic personality who served from 1959 to 1972, (d) the active people come in disproportionately large numbers from among the members who joined most recently, and (e) there is a sizable cadre of active and

very loyal people who have been members for more than a quarter
of a century—many of whom have changed their place of residence
two or three times since they united with this congregation.

TENURE OF TODAY'S MEMBERS

	Active	Inactive	Total
Joined before 1950	12%	6%	18%
Joined 1950-59	8%	5%	13%
Joined 1960-69	10%	10%	20%
Joined 1970-79	16%	8%	24%
Joined 1980-84	22%	3%	25%
Total	68%	32%	100%

The tenure pattern in the typical suburban church would show a
much larger proportion of newer members, a lower proportion of
inactive members and far fewer members who joined before 1950.
What is the tenure picture for your congregation? How do you
interpret those figures?

8

Who Are Our Members?

 In addition to a review of membership trends, the self-appraisal committee usually will find it helpful to examine the characteristics of today's congregation. Four different sets of questions about the characteristics of today's members can be very rewarding.

The Church Attendance Survey

The most useful, and, naturally, the most work is a survey of church attendance covering four consecutive Sundays. In most states May and October are "average" months for church attendance (Florida and Arizona are notable exceptions!).[1] The value of an attendance survey can be illustrated by looking at two examples. The first compares three congregations, each with approximately five hundred confirmed members and each with an attendance at Sunday morning worship that averaged two hundred thirty for the year. On first glance these three congregations appear to be similar.

An attendance survey, however, pointed up some important distinctions that helped each congregation plan more knowledgeably for today and tomorrow.

Some of these differences can be seen by looking at this table that summarized the results of an attendance survey conducted over four consecutive Sundays. (See table on following page.)

What did this attendance survey reveal?

First, it revealed a very sharp difference in church-going patterns among the members of the three congregations. In Church A, 83 percent of the members were present for corporate worship at least once during the four-week survey period, while in Church B that figure was 61 percent, but in Church C it was only 46 percent.

These differences pointed up a division in Church C that many people had been trying to ignore in various ways. One man, for example, had dismissed it with the comment, "Everyone knows that half of the church members in this country *never* attend worship."

This is simply not true. While the proportion of members who will attend worship at least one Sunday a month tends to decrease as the membership total rises, in the typical Protestant congregation with 300 to 600 resident confirmed members, approximately 60 to 80 percent of the members will attend worship at least once during the average month and 40 to 70 percent will attend at least twice. According to the Gallup Poll, on an average Sunday approximately 40 percent of all Protestant church members in the United States will attend worship. When over one-half of the members of a five-hundred-member parish do not attend even once in the average month, this is often a sign of trouble. (In some smaller denominational families such as the Missionary Church and the Christian Reformed Church, more than nine out of ten members will be at worship on the average Sunday morning.)

CHURCH ATTENDANCE SURVEY

	Church A	Church B	Church C
Resident confirmed membership	493	518	501
Member attendance (by persons)	414	317	232
One Sunday	189	61	18
Two Sundays	108	111	37
Three Sundays	80	76	74
Four Sundays	37	69	103
Non-member attendance (average per Sunday)			
Children of members	4	16	45
Constituents	9	4	3
Visitors	19	14	2

The attendance survey simply reflected a deep split in Church C. Approximately one-third of the members had become offended over an internal personality conflict and had lapsed into almost complete inactivity. Since this was a congregation with a large number of children in attendance at the worship service, this division was not reflected in the total attendance figure.

Church C also has an intensely loyal core of members who form a closely knit fellowship. This "faction" has dominated the life of this parish for years and it consists of about sixty families. These sixty families, with their teen-age children and a few grandparents, account for nearly all the members in attendance on the typical Sunday. The "wall" this group has built around the church is indicated by (a) the large number of members who did not attend even once, (b) the relatively few members who attended once or twice a month, and (c) the remarkably low number of visitors.

A second important point revealed by this attendance survey concerns Church A. This parish has a high degree of visibility, it tends to attract a comparatively large number of visitors, it has an outstanding program for identifying and contacting visitors, and it receives an average of nearly one hundred new confirmed members each year, but it has not done a very good job in assimilating these new members into the life of the congregation. This was hinted at by the relatively large number of members who attended only once or twice a month and the small proportion attending three or four times in the survey month.

The attendance survey documented the urgency of emphasizing *both* outreach and assimilation in the evangelism program at Church A.

The attendance pattern at Church B is more typical, but the results stimulated the leaders to raise three questions that they decided demanded immediate attention.

First, two hundred resident members did not attend even once during the survey month. Why?

Second, if there was an average of fourteen visitors each Sunday, who was following up on these contacts?

Third, since this parish identified itself as emphasizing a "family worship service" and encouraged the entire family to attend worship together, why was there an average of only sixteen children of pre-confirmation age at worship on the typical Sunday? The attendance survey suggests the self-image of the parish does not coincide with reality. Why?

A second example of the value of an attendance survey is revealed by this one taken at a downtown church in a city of

30,000. One-half of the members of this 980-confirmed-member church united with that congregation before 1973 and one-half joined in 1973 or later. Each person in attendance at either of the two Sunday morning services was asked to fill out a 3 x 5 inch survey card that looked like this:

CHURCH ATTENDANCE SURVEY

Name_____

Check one:

    Member_____   Constituent_____

    Child_____   Visitor_____

If a member, check one:

    Joined before 1973_____

    Joined in 1973 or later_____

Check one: Female_____   Male_____

Blue cards were passed out on the first Sunday, pink the second, yellow the third, and white the fourth. This facilitated the work of the volunteers who tabulated the cards. The use of colors eliminated any possible confusion over which Sunday was represented by a particular card. A card was to be filled out for each person present, regardless of age. The ushers were asked to make a careful and complete head count each Sunday to provide a comparison base for determining the proportion of attenders who filled out attendance cards.

Several findings emerged from this attendance survey. First, the coverage was good, but not complete. A card was turned in for approximately 82 percent of those in attendance each week. Second, while one-half of the members joined before 1973, these long-time members accounted for 59.3 percent of the members attending at least once. That raises a question about the capability of this large church to assimilate the newer members.

Third, this survey revealed that 61 percent of those attending at least once were female and 39 percent were male. This surprised some since the confirmed membership was 55 percent female and 45 percent male. (In the United States 53 percent of all persons age twenty-one and over are female.) In 1952 the worship attendance in mainline Protestant churches was approximately 53 percent female and 47 percent male. In 1965 the ratio was 55-45 and in 1982 approximately 59-41.

CHURCH ATTENDANCE SURVEY

May 1, 8, 15, 22

	Joined before 1973	Joined 1973 or later	Total
Members attending one Sunday	94	87	181
Members attending two Sundays	112	70	182
Members attending three Sundays	94	58	152
Members attending four Sundays	56	33	89
Members attending at least once	356	248	604

Percentage of female members attending at least once—61%
Percentage of male members attending at least once—39%

Average number of visitors	17
Average number of constituents	14
Average number of children	26
Usher count of attendance (average)	482

Fourth, only 604 of the 980 confirmed members, or 62 percent, attended even once. This is an especially significant figure since a great effort had been made to "clean up the membership rolls." Two years earlier nearly three hundred names had been removed by action of the governing board. While large churches usually have a lower participation rate than smaller congregations, the fact that 376 confirmed members did not attend even once in a month that included both Mother's Day and Confirmation Sunday should be a cause of concern.

Fifth, the "regulars," those attending three or four of the four Sundays, were outnumbered by the "irregulars," those attending only once or twice, by 363 to 241, a 3-to-2 ratio. To be more precise, the membership in that particular month divided itself into three groups, with the largest group composed of those who did not attend even once in that four-Sunday period.

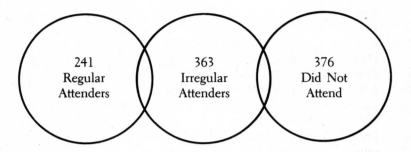

Sixth, of the 248 members joining in 1973 or later who attended at least once during that four-week period, only 37 percent came on three or four Sundays. This contrasts with the 356 "oldtimers" who attended at least once. Out of that latter group 43 percent attended on three or four Sundays. This reinforces the point made earlier that the assimilation processes were somewhat ineffective during the 1970s and early 1980s.

Finally, if "regular" is defined as twice a month or oftener, 423 members, or 43 percent, could be classified as regular attenders. This is a disturbingly low proportion!

How does the worship attendance in your congregation compare with these patterns?

Where Do Our Members Live?

In addition to this statistical tabulation, it often is helpful to spot the place of residence of each attender on a map. A blue dot may represent each member attending three or four Sundays, a red dot for each member attending twice, a green dot for each member attending once, and a yellow dot for a visitor. Be sure to use one dot for each person. Do not use one for a family! The best way to do this is with colored ink. The second best method is to use colored paste-on dots. The poorest procedure is to use colored pins, since they tend to make it very difficult to move or store the map.

In most parishes a map showing the place of residence of *attenders* provides a much more meaningful picture of the geographical shape of the parish than does a map showing the place of residence of families. For the benefit of those persons who are convinced an effective self-appraisal requires the preparation of several spot maps, the six most useful maps usually will be (a) a map showing the place of residence of all adults uniting with this congregation during the past two or three years, (b) a map showing the place of residence of all regular attenders at worship, (c) a map showing the place of residence of all inactive members, (d) a map showing the current place of residence of all babies born to members during the past two years, (e) a map showing the last place of permanent residence of each member who died during the past two years, and (f) a map showing the place of residence of each officer or leader of that congregation. It often helps to compare these last three maps.

When you have completed the membership survey, there are several questions that automatically will come to mind as you look at the table summarizing the data and the map showing the geographical distribution of the attenders.

Many more questions will come to mind if you compare the results of an attendance survey in your parish with similar studies made in other nearby or similar congregations.

The Family and Marital Status

One of the more useful questions to raise in a congregational self-analysis concerns the family and marital status of the adult (age eighteen and over) members. This can be illustrated by looking at the tabulation for the seven-hundred-forty confirmed-member Grace Lutheran Church located in a growing suburban city of forty thousand residents in a metropolitan area of over three million people.

From this effort the leaders at Grace discovered (a) three-quarters of the adult members are married and living with their spouse, an above-average proportion, (b) the parish includes twice as many widowed women as would be expected on the basis of the community population, (c) Grace Church is not reaching single men, (d) the membership includes twenty-seven currently divorced women—this figure astonished the members of the self-appraisal committee since most thought it was a single digit number—but it would have been over forty if Grace had included a representative cross section of the residents of that community, and (e) perhaps most significant of all, less than one-half of the adult members are part of a husband-wife couple family with children under the age of eighteen still at home. Before this study was undertaken all of the policy makers at Grace had assumed this was predominantly a "family parish" with most of the members living in homes that included a husband and wife with children under eighteen years of age. That was and is an accurate description of the policy makers—and most of the others had fit into that category up until the youngest child had left home a few years earlier.

FAMILY AND MARITAL STATUS

(Resident adult members age 18 and over)

	Grace	Community	U.S.
Husbands and wives living together with children under 18 at home	46%	44%	32%
Husbands and wives without children under 18 at home	29%	26%	31%
Single men	4%	9%	11%
Single women	10%	9%	9%
Currently divorced women	4%	6%	4%
Currently divorced men	1%	1%	3%
Currently separated from spouse	1%	3%	3%
Currently widowed women	4%	2%	7%
Currently widowed men	1%	*	1%

Total resident members age 18 and over = **683**

*Less than one-half of 1 percent of the males in that community were widowed.

Those leaders who insist that the top priority should be on a ministry with families that consist of a husband-wife couple with children under eighteen should note that (a) less than one-third of all adults in the United States fit into that category, (b) the number of families that fit into that category *decreased* by 606,000 between 1970 and 1981, and (c) the number of single-parent families increased by three million between 1970 and 1981, and they now constitute one out of five families that include children under eighteen at home.

What is the family and marital status of the members of your congregation? Do the facts match the assumptions? What do the facts say to the priorities in programming, to the allocation of resources, and to the growth strategy of your parish?

The Age Distribution

The third of these four questions to ask about today's members concerns the age mix. In doing this it is helpful to use the age brackets adopted by the Bureau of the Census rather than the traditional five-year age cohorts that do not follow the grade system of most public schools. In other words, rather than lump the ten-to fourteen-year-old group together, it may be better to use a fourteen-to seventeen-year-old category that coincides with the four-year high school.

This table compares the age mix of a one-hundred-twenty-year-old downtown First Baptist Church (FBC) with the age distribution of the American population in 1980. The self-study committee discovered (a) the median age of the baptized membership was fifty-eight years old, (b) only one-tenth of the baptized membership were under twenty-five years of age, (c) only 1 percent of the members were of high school age, and (d) nearly two out of every five members had passed their sixty-fifth birthday.

THE AGE MIX

Age	FBC	USA	Age	FBC	USA
0-13	3%	21%	35-44	11%	11%
14-17	1%	7%	45-54	10%	10%
18-21	2%	8%	55-64	18%	10%
22-24	4%	6%	65-74	20%	7%
25-34	13%	16%	75 & over	18%	4%

This statistical summary provided a useful context for the issue that divided the members of the committee. Should we make our number one priority employing a youth director who can build up our ministry with high school age young people and our number two priority getting a children's worker who can rebuild the children's department of the Sunday school? Approximately one-half of the committee supported that position. The other half argued, "Look, we're a downtown church composed largely of mature adults. Less than half of our members are currently married. Let's specialize in what we can do. Let's make our ministry with mature adults our number one priority and specialize in a ministry with persons who live alone. Four out of five Baptist churches in this county are trying to be family-centered churches. Perhaps God is calling us to use our central location downtown to reach the folks most churches overlook or ignore."

How would such a debate come out in your church? What does the age distribution of your members say to your priorities? Do you prefer to place the top priority in "filling in the weaknesses" or in "reinforcing strengths"?

The Use of Subjective Data

Finally, a word should be added about some useful data that are more difficult to obtain. Topping this list is the denominational background of each adult member (age eighteen and over) and especially of recent adult new members. What proportion of your members have always been members of this parish? Of this denomination? What proportion of adults joined this congregation as new Christians? What proportion came from another church in this denomination? From another church in a different denomination? How many married into this parish? How many are the second or third generation from that family to be members here?

Contrary to conventional wisdom, in most numerically growing churches, the majority of today's adult members (a) did not grow up in this congregation, (b) do not have kinfolk in this parish, and (c) have not been members of this denominational family all of their lives. The majority of rapidly growing churches today draw most of their members from (a) adults who are new Christians and (b) adults who previously had been members of a church of a different denominational family.

In many sections of the country a second question should be, How many of our adult new members were reared in the Roman Catholic Church? One of the big reversals from the 1950s is this migration. In the 1950s three-quarters of the Catholic-non-Catholic marriages produced a new member for a Catholic parish. Today one-fourth of those marriages produces a new member for a Catholic parish.[2]

In 1982 the typical Protestant congregation reported that approximately 15 percent of its adult new members had been reared Roman Catholic, and it is not unusual to find congregations in which that figure is in the 30 to 50 percent range. The most obvious reason is the issue of birth control, but the teachings of the Catholic Church on divorce and remarriage, the authoritarian structure, and the refusal to ordain women also are factors.

A distant third on this list are questions about the level of educational attainment, the status of members in the labor force (professional, laborer), and the socioeconomic class of each member. While many of the traditional self-study guides ask for these data, they are very difficult to determine and of questionable value. The origins of those questions can be traced back to the 1920s when there were very significant differences among the several social classes. One of these differences was in church attendance. In the 1920s Protestant churches were far more oriented toward the "business class" and less toward the working class.[3] Today the cultural homogeneity and the broadened outreach of the churches reduce the relevance of such questions. A few sentences on this subject may be of value in the material that is prepared by the pulpit search committee, but the value usually is more apparent than real.

Perhaps the most useful of these subjective questions, but also the most difficult to answer, would be a summary identifying where each member is in his or her religious pilgrimage.[4] In at least a few churches this has been a tremendous asset in expanding the adult Christian education program, in enabling the preacher to speak to the people's needs, in reducing unproductive conflict, and in improving internal communication.

What Should We Omit?

Conspicuous by their absence in this chapter are suggestions that data be secured on (a) the characteristics of the residents who live near the church building, (b) the proportion of members who live within one mile or one-half mile of the meeting place, (c) the location of the buildings housing other congregations, and (d) the distribution of the membership by gender (if this is done a useful exercise would be part of the survey of worship attendance, not membership).

Some of the reasons for those omissions can be found in several of the operational assumptions of this writer.

First, the concept of the geographical parish began to disappear with the increase in the ownership and use of the private automobile.

The American Catholic Church began to recognize that fact of life in the 1950s, but many white Protestant leaders continued to urge congregations to see themselves as geographical parishes and/or to reestablish themselves as geographical parishes. The two largest products of this emphasis on a geographical concept of ministry were frustration and guilt. Black, Asian, and Hispanic church leaders are now beginning to understand that and an increasing number are able to affirm it.

A second and related operational assumption is this is a free country, more or less, and people will make a choice of where they go to church on the basis of which congregation can meet their needs, not on the basis of geographical proximity. Therefore the emphasis in this book is on identifying and being responsive to people's needs, not on convenience. What happens, or does not happen, within that congregation is far more influential in shaping its future, determining its vitality and in affecting its outreach than what happens in neighboring churches!

A third operational assumption runs contrary to conventional wisdom and is based on a growing body of very persuasive evidence that suggests (a) the congregation that has a denominational monopoly in that community tends to be weaker and/or less effective than when a sister church of the same denomination meets in a nearby building (this may not be a cause-and-effect relationship) and (b) more people go to church in communities, such as Muncie, Indiana,[5] and other places where there is at least one religious congregation for every five hundred to a thousand residents than go to worship in places, such as San Francisco and New York, where there are relatively few religious congregations per one hundred thousand residents. Again it is not possible to prove a cause-and-effect relationship but church growth studies consistently show church attendance is higher in places where there are many religious congregations per ten thousand residents. In other words, people should not be scared of shadows or of the shadows of nearby church buildings.

Finally, persuasive evidence can be gathered to suggest that most congregations, both Protestant and Catholic, are increasingly oriented toward women and away from men. Therefore the sharp increase in the proportion of worship attenders who are female should surprise no one. Until an effort is made to strengthen the appeal to men, that trend probably will continue.[6] In addition to counting people by gender, it may also be useful to examine the bias in the program and outreach of that congregation.

9

WHAT IS THE MODEL
OF CONGREGATIONAL LIFE?

"Reverend Baylor knew everyone and he attracted new members just as honey draws flies," reflected Henry Newman, a lifelong member of the seven-hundred-member church. "I would guess that he was personally responsible for at least two-thirds of the people who are members here today."

"It might even be a higher proportion than that," agreed Hazel White. "My husband used to say he was like flypaper. I guess no one should be surprised that our attendance has dropped off here since he retired after twenty-six years as our minister. A lot of people had close ties to him."

The Pastor-Centered Model

These comments reflect a common model of congregational life. This pastor-centered model frequently is the result of a long pastorate spanning two or three or four decades by an attractive, person-centered, extroverted, hardworking and charming minister who is skilled at being able to call everyone by name. The dominant dynamic of congregational life is the very large number of one-to-one relationships between that minister and individual members. A much less visible component of this model is the modest emphasis on building other ties between the congregation and the individual members. Many laypeople are attracted by this model of congregational life. Everyone enjoys being known personally and loved by the pastor. In larger congregations averaging two hundred or more at worship this is a relatively low cost model since expenditures for additional staff can be kept to a minimum. Nearly every pastoral change is disruptive and this model minimizes the number of disruptions per quarter century. The responsibility for recruiting new members is carried largely by the pastor, thus reducing the work of the laity. When a member dies, the family is reassured by the fact that the clergyperson officiating at that funeral service knew the deceased very well. Parents appreciate it when the same minister is available to baptize the new baby, subsequently confirm that child as a member, eventually officiate at the wedding and perhaps be there to baptize the first grandchild. All of us are more comfortable with continuity than with discontinuity. The lay leaders become accustomed to a style of ministerial leadership and do not have to learn and adjust to a new style every few years. The more observant members note this model of congregational life often is unusually effective at maintaining an intergenerational mix in the membership. The only gap in the age distribution may be in the active participation of the sixteen to thirty age bracket.

Pastor-Centered Church

PUFF! PUFF!

"Some churches run on the energy of a persuasive-powerful pastor!" —FRIAR TUCK

The big disadvantage of this model of congregational life, of course, can be summarized in one question. What happens if the pastor dies, retires, resigns, or runs off with a member of the choir? For most members this is a moot question. It has not happened yet and no one expects it will happen in the foreseeable future.

The Unifying-Goal Model

"The fire was the best thing that ever happened to this congregation," declared Frank Heath. "We had been drifting along for years, mostly fighting with or over a series of preachers who came and went, when our whole church was destroyed by fire. Everyone pitched in and in less than two years we had completely rebuilt the church and then we concentrated our attention on paying off the indebtedness. At last month's board meeting we were told that we can be debt-free in another fifteen to eighteen months if everybody continues to cooperate. I've been a member here for over forty years and I've never seen the sense of unity in this congregation that we have here today!"

the **Central** goal Model

HERE, *the* PASTOR HOPES THEY WON'T LOWER THEIR SIGHTS! (GULP!)

"Other churches gain because of their aim!"

—— FRIAR TUCK.

"My dad always said a church does its best when it has a mortgage," chimed in Helen Cole. "I guess we're proving that old piece of wisdom still applies, even though the world has changed a lot since his time."

These comments illustrate a second model of congregational life. The central dynamic is the presence of specific, attainable, measurable, highly visible, unifying and satisfaction-producing goals. In some congregations it is constructing a new meeting place or paying off a mortgage or recovering from the damages resulting from a natural disaster such as a fire or a flood or a tornado or a hurricane. Sometimes this model is represented by the pastor who carries the reputation, "Wherever he goes he always sees the need for a building program. He is a builder. If you need a new building, get him for your next pastor." That pastor, perhaps without realizing it, seems to impose this model of congregational life on every congregation he serves.

In other congregations a parallel model of congregational life is represented by the fact that over half of the annual expenditures go for the support of missionaries, several of whom come out of this church. The missionary challenge is the single unifying goal. During the last half of the nineteenth century and the first six decades of the twentieth century the expansion of the Sunday school was the central unifying goal for tens of thousands of congregations. A few churches have made the nurturing of new congregations that central unifying goal.

The Three-Circle Model

"Our members can be divided into three groups," explained the minister of the two-hundred-member congregation located in a small town of nearly eighteen hundred residents. "One-third come to church practically every Sunday, one-third take turns coming or staying away and one-third come on Easter and Christmas if they don't have anything else to do."

"That's something like what we have over at our church," observed the recently arrived pastor at Calvary Church. "We have the oldtimers who remember the years they spent in the building over on Adams Street, we have another group who sparked the relocation and the construction of our new building, and we have the people who have joined since the new building was completed." As he spoke he walked over and sketched three circles on the chalkboard. "Our outer circle is composed of the oldtimers, many of whom used to be in the inner circle. The current inner circle is composed largely of a group of people who provided the leadership for the relocation effort."

The Three Circle Model

NEW MEMBERS
OLD
CURRENT
CORE
TIMERS
LESS ACTIVE

*"Some churches read like a book
with a beginning, middle
and the current
climax!"*

—FRIAR TUCK.

These two pastors are describing a third model of congregational life. It is based on the assumption, usually unspoken, that every congregation can be conceptualized as consisting of three circles. One minister used it to describe the congregation she is serving. "We have three groups in our congregation, those who are still opposed to the idea of a woman minister, those who favor the ordination of women, and those who are more concerned about good preaching than about gender."

One Lutheran pastor said, "I am serving three congregations, the oldtimers who had a strong allegiance to the old Augustana Synod, those who identify themselves as Lutherans but have no strong allegiance to any Synod, and a third group who had never been Lutherans before joining this parish."

The Small-Group Model

During an afternoon break at a workshop for leaders in Christian education one participant was explaining to a new friend, "The greatest thing that has happened in our congregation has been the expansion of our Bible study program beyond Sunday morning.

We used to have three adult Bible groups that met during the church school hour on Sunday morning. Four years ago we went into a systematic program to train people to teach a new curriculum. Now we have nine groups that meet on various evenings during the week plus two new groups that meet on Sunday morning. When you add these fourteen Bible study groups to the five circles in the women's organization, the senior high youth fellowship, our women's prayer circle, the Christian education committee which really is a mutual support group, the three Caring-Sharing groups, and the other groups we have such as the adult handbell choir, the youth choir, and the chancel choir plus the Mother's Club, it all adds up to more than thirty groups that meet on a continuous basis. That's not bad for a four-hundred-member church, is it?"

That is not bad. In fact, it is remarkable! The typical four-hundred member congregation will have no more than twelve to twenty adult and youth groups that meet on a regular basis.

The Small Group Model

"For other churches,
it's the wheels
within the wheels
that keep them rolling!"
—FRIAR TUCK

That describes a fourth model of congregational life. It may also be the most discussed and highly visible model. It has been the subject of scores of books that have advocated the strengthening of the group life as the most productive road to congregational renewal.[1]

One version is to build the group life around a series of Bible study classes. Another version is the "undershepherd" or "zone" or "parish" plan. This involves dividing the congregation into a series of smaller units, usually on the basis of the place of residence of the members, and assigning a zone leader or undershepherd to each of these subgroups. This usually turns out to be a high cost venture in terms of time, energy, and supervision. A huge amount of effort is required to make sure that everyone in that passing parade of members is an active member of a zone and that the zone leaders carry out their responsibilities.

The most widespread version is responsive to the differences among people and to the fact that few people socialize primarily with their geographical neighbors. In this version of the small-group model, individual interests and concerns, rather than the member's place of residence, is the central organizing principle in creating small groups. This version includes all the classes, circles, choirs, cells, fellowships, committees, and organizations in which the members enjoy being a part of that group. (The next chapter suggests methods for evaluating and strengthening the group life of your congregation.)

The Common-Heritage Model

"Everyone here seems to be related to someone else in the congregation," explained the Reverend Susan Miller, the recently arrived minister at Covenant Church to an old friend from college and seminary who had dropped by to spend an hour or two with Susan. "The first thing I've had to learn is to be very careful when talking about people. That's not how it was in the suburban church I grew up in before I went away to college. Everyone I meet here is someone's relative. Last night I mentioned this at the council meeting and it turned out that all but two members of the council were related to at least one other person in the room. That's a new experience for me."

That also is an example of a fifth model of congregational life. It is the common-heritage model. One version, which Susan Miller encountered, is the kinfolk tie. The central dynamic in congregational life is the network of kinfolk ties that the members have with one another. Another version is the Korean congregation in which nearly all of the adult members are persons who were born in Korea and moved to Canada or to the United States after 1955.

The Common Heritage Model

"Some churches run on the momentum of their original uniqueness!"

— FRIAR TUCK

A generation or two ago the Augustana Lutheran parish or the Cumberland Presbyterian Church or the "Old" Mennonite Church or the Swedish Covenant Church or the German Baptist congregation or the Presbyterian Church in Canada or the Finnish Lutheran parish also were examples of this common-heritage model of congregational life. Everyone was aware of a shared heritage that was a strong cohesive and unifying thread. Sometimes it was primarily nationality and language. Sometimes it was primarily doctrinal and the nationality tie was a secondary cohesive force.

Today the common-heritage churches appear to be declining in numbers as a distinctive model of congregational life, but many people in the Christian Reformed Church or the Conservative Congregational Christian Conference or the Church of the Lutheran Confession or various Amish sects or the Missionary Church might disagree with that generalization.

The Congregation-of-Congregations Model

"The best way to understand Redeemer Church is to begin with the fact that we have three worship services every weekend," explained a prominent layman from that fourteen-hundred-member congregation. "The Saturday evening service usually draws between fifty and seventy-five, the eight-thirty morning service averages close to three hundred and the eleven o'clock service is the largest with between four hundred and five hundred on the typical Sunday. Even though we offer people these three choices, nearly all of the regular attenders come to the same hour week after week. About the only difference is that in the summer some of the folks who usually attend on Sunday morning occasionally go to the Saturday evening service."

Redeemer Church is an example of the trend to offer people more choices. It also illustrates a sixth model of congregational life.

The churches that have institutionalized this schedule can be described as a congregation-of-congregations. Most of the regular attenders usually have a strong attachment to the people who gather at a particular hour for the corporate worship of God. It is not unusual for a member to observe, "We belong to the Saturday night crowd," or "We're a part of the eight-thirty congregation." While the details vary greatly from one parish to another, the small group life and the social fellowship often reflect these worship attendance lines. In a few congregations one minister is the regular preacher for the first service and another pastor is the regular preacher for the late service. This not only increases the total attendance, it also reinforces the loyalties of the members to a particular hour for worship.

These six examples illustrate the concept of several different models of how congregational life is organized. While most churches fit into one of these six categories, or perhaps a combination of two models, two notable exceptions should be mentioned before asking what the implications may be.

The first exception consists of those churches that are organized around some other central unifying principle. One example is the congregation that identified and organized against the enemy. A common illustration is the minister who comes into the community and organizes a new congregation on the grounds that all other self-identified Christian churches are really agents of the devil. A second example can be found in the hundreds of small rural congregations that built their life as a community around a deep attachment to that place—the sacred building and the cemetery next to the building. In a few denominations the distinctive dimension of congregational life is the liturgy. The self-identified Anglo-Catholic parish in the Episcopal Church is an example. While it is less common than it was in the 1920s before the homogenizing of social class distinctions had taken place,[2] there still remains a significant number of Protestant churches in which social class is the distinctive characteristic of congregational life. Today these churches are more common among the lower class than among upper-class Protestants.[3]

The second exception to the central theme of this chapter is the passive church. Many of these congregations no longer display a distinctive model of congregational life. Most of them are at a stage in which they have completed a chapter in their history that resembles one of the six models described here, but have yet to agree on a new model. Typically they have drifted into a passive state that is expressed by a lack of widespread agreement on role, direction, or goals.[4] They are in a passive search for a new model of congregational life.

Which of these models describes your congregation today? How does this model compare with the model that fit your congregation a decade ago? If they are different, what are the implications of the changes? Has a change of pastors changed the model? Has a change of models influenced the redefinition of the role and responsibilities of the pastor and/or of other paid staff members? What are some of the implications of today's model for program development? For leadership development? For expanding the evangelistic outreach? For enhancing the sense of community outreach? For facilitating the assimilation of new members?

10
How Is the Group Life?

"It used to be that when I walked in on Sunday morning I knew everybody. I could even call all of the children by name," lamented Henry Johnson. "In those days we were one big family. In the last few years, however, our church has grown so rapidly that I doubt if I could identify more than a third of the folks by name. There's another group that I recognize, but I can't call by name and I suppose there's at least a couple of dozen whom, if I met them on the street during the week, I wouldn't recognize and I expect they wouldn't know me either."

"Up until my husband died eight years ago I had always been involved in small churches where I knew everyone. Five years ago, when I moved here to be near my daughter and her family, I knew I could never be happy in a big church such as this one," reflected Opal Henderson, a sixty-three-year-old widow. "I was wrong! I've been a circle leader for the past two years. I am also active in an adult Sunday school class. I sing in the choir and I'm always here from nine to three on Tuesday for our quilting group. While I doubt if I know even a fourth of the members here, each of these groups is a kind of a church within the church. That's where I've met all my friends."

"My wife and I go to the eight-thirty service on Sunday morning," explained Clark Brennan. "We have a baby who gets us up early, so we go to that early service. In the six months we've been here about the only people we've met are the folks who come to that first service and, of course, the people in our couples' Sunday school class."

Those three comments illustrate one of the most significant differences among small churches, middle-sized congregations, and the really big parishes. The small congregation usually functions as "one big family" or as an overgrown small group. The primary relationships of the members are to one another. Frequently kinfolk ties are influential in reinforcing various

133

relationships and in determining who may be eligible for certain offices. If the small congregation doubles or triples in size, however, it becomes very difficult for many of the oldtimers to expand that friendship circle sufficiently to include all the newcomers. When strangers become a majority of that friendship circle, many of the oldtimers feel overwhelmed and some begin to feel like outsiders.

The middle-sized congregation of several hundred members may appear to be huge to the widow who has spent all her life in small churches, but if it has an extensive group life, she can find a home there within two or three or four of these face-to-face groups. She may never know more than a small fraction of the total membership by name, but she will find it easy to meet and make new friends in a circle or the choir or in an adult class or a sewing group. These closely knit groups often are described as a "church within the church." That should be seen as a positive statement, not as a criticism.

The large congregation with two or three worship services on Sunday morning, and perhaps an alternative worship experience on Thursday or Saturday or Monday evening, is a far more complex organization. It frequently becomes a congregation-of-congregations. Some members are perceived as "belonging to the eleven o'clock service." Others are "a part of the eight-thirty crowd" and still others are the "Thursday evening group." The senior pastor sometimes is reminded of those three years right after seminary when he or she served a three-church parish. It is not at all uncommon for one adult Sunday school class to be drawn entirely from those who usually attend the eleven o'clock service while one circle in the women's organization is composed largely of women who attend the first service and the two others are drawn largely from among those attending at eleven o'clock.

These three patterns of congregational group life can be represented by the diagram on the following page.

The small membership church has one large inner friendship circle. The small congregation often consists of three groups of people, (a) those who belong to that inner circle, (b) those who are members, but do not feel a part of that inner circle, and (c) those who are not officially members, but who identify with that congregation if and when they feel the need of a church.

<table>
<tr><td></td><td>The Middle-sized</td><td></td></tr>
<tr><td>The Small Church</td><td>Congregation</td><td>The Large Church</td></tr>
</table>

The middle-sized congregation includes that large circle of members, but most of those with a strong feeling of belonging are a part of a face-to-face group such as the choir, the governing board, a prayer circle, a Bible study group, the Christian education committee, the deacons, the task force on evangelism, a circle in the women's organization, a thirty-six-week new member's orientation class, a Bethel class, or the trustees.

The large congregation, as suggested earlier, may resemble a congregation-of-congregations, each with its own loyal followers. In one Lutheran parish one congregation is composed of a small group of mature adults plus a few recent newcomers from Germany who always attend the eight-thirty German language service. Another distinctive group is composed of adults who are lifelong members or who married a lifelong member. Most of these are second or third generation members of that parish. Worshiping with them at that second service, which *always* is in English, are the newer members who do not have kinfolk in this parish. In effect, that second worship service includes two "congregations." Most of the policy makers come from the second of these three "congregations," but two elderly men, both of whom usually attend the German service, still have considerable influence, although neither one is in any official leadership office. The last time the pastor checked, he was surprised to discover that nearly one-half of the workers (Sunday school teachers, choir members, youth counselors) came from that third congregation of recent new members. One of the tension points is the disapproval frequently expressed by members of that second congregation toward ideas suggested by the newcomers who "belong" to that third congregation.

Bethany, a large suburban parish founded in 1957, includes four identifiable congregations. The smallest is composed of the pioneers who clearly recall "back when we met in the school for nearly three years." A second congregation is composed of those who joined during the nineteen-year pastorate of the Reverend Harrison, the second minister to serve that congregation, and the one who had the longest pastorate of any minister ever to serve at Bethany. Nearly all of them also were members at the time of the fire that destroyed most of the "new building." A third congregation is composed of those who joined after the rebuilding program had been completed, but before Dr. Harrison's departure. The newest congregation, and of course the only one that is growing in numbers, is composed of those newcomers who have no firsthand recollection of the fire, the rebuilding, or of the Reverend Harrison. But it is hard for many of the oldtimers to accept the fact that the future of Bethany rests with the members of this fourth congregation—and of a fifth and sixth congregation that have yet to emerge.

One source of the friction at Bethany today is the "new minister" who persists in trying to change things "from the way Dr. Harrison always did it." A related source of tension is the support this new senior pastor and the new associate minister are getting from all those new people who are coming to Bethany. Many of them do not comprehend the dismay caused by that fire and the way the members sacrificed to rebuild. Some do not even appear to understand this is a sacred building.

Another source of anxiety at Bethany is the numerical decline of the Couples Class. This was the first adult Sunday school class to be organized while the new congregation was still meeting in the school. For two decades a large proportion of the influential lay leadership came from the Couples Class. Since the fire the class has declined by nearly one-third in size and the Pathfinders Class is now the biggest single source of influential leaders. The second largest class is the Homebuilders, composed largely of younger parents and recently married couples, but it is not yet a center of congregational power. Most of the members of the Pathfinders

Class attend the nine-thirty worship service while nearly all of the Couples Class worship at eleven o'clock. Several of the oldtimers wonder if the two new ministers are not directing most of the new members—some of whom would be fine additions to the Couples Class—to the Pathfinders Class or to the Homebuilders Class.

Just because they share the same roof and the same staff it does not automatically follow that the several congregations in the large church will be free of rivalries and jealousies.

This introduction to the concept provides the context for suggesting a half dozen questions that can be used to appraise the group life of your congregation.

The Number and Variety

Typically the hundred-member congregation needs six to seven different, but overlapping, face-to-face groups such as the choir, an adult Sunday school class, the Christian education committee, the governing board, and the women's organization to accommodate that many members.

What qualifies as one of these groups? The basic criteria are (a) the group includes fewer than thirty-five persons (five to seven is best, eight to seventeen is second best, and eighteen to thirty-five is a distant third), (b) the majority of the members find it a rewarding experience to be a member of that group, (c) many of the participants have made close personal friends from within that group, (d) the group meets weekly or at least monthly, and (e) participation in that group makes an important contribution to the personal and spiritual growth of most of the members.

It is not uncommon to find six or seven of these groups in the hundred-member church. It is far less likely that one will be able to identify sixty to seventy face-to-face groups in the thousand-member congregation. The most common products of an inadequate number of face-to-face groups include (a) a disproportionately large number of members become inactive, (b) many of the new members have difficulty in gaining a sense of belonging, (c) difficulties are experienced in enlisting volunteers and it appears the burden of serving as workers and leaders "falls on the same old loyal core," (d) members find it easy to drop out or switch their membership to another church whenever there is an internal disruption, (e) new members often have a strong loyalty to the minister and drop out when that minister leaves, (f) the teaching ministry of that congregation is inadequate to meet the needs of all the people, (g) means-to-an-end issues such as real estate, finances, and personnel tend to dominate the agenda of the governing board, and (h) the pressures and strains of pluralism become increasingly divisive.

How many face-to-face groups do you have for each one hundred members?

The second half of this question concerns the increasing demand by people for choices. What choices do you offer people? This point can be illustrated by three examples.

In an increasing number of congregations the women's organization includes several *different* circles. At Central Church two are Bible study circles, one is a mission study circle, one focuses on a tutoring program in an inner-city school, one is a book review circle, one accepts the leadership for planning next year's bazaar, one is a support group for the seminary library two hundred miles away, two focus on calling on shut-ins (one on lonely persons in the county nursing home and the other on members who are shut-ins), one is for young mothers, another is for mothers who have a handicapped son or daughter, the members of one circle sew for charitable organizations, and one is the liturgical dance group. Several women are active participants in two or three of these circles. This contrasts with the tradition that every circle is a study group that studies the same material; the basic difference is that one meets in the morning, three in the afternoon, and two in the evening.

A second example is the ministry with youth that includes two different high school age Sunday school classes, a youth choir, an early Tuesday morning Bible study and prayer breakfast, a Sunday evening youth fellowship, a handbell choir, a week-long summer mission work camp experience, a twice-a-year religious drama presentation, and a series of summer camp experiences. Many of the youth participate in all of them. This contrasts with the traditional concept of the four choices of (a) a Sunday school class, (b) a youth fellowship, (c) a youth choir, and (d) none of the above with the majority of the high school age youth choosing the fourth alternative.

A third example is the church that offers five different adult classes on Sunday morning—one for couples, one for widows, one with a discussion format, one that is primarily a lecture class, and one that is a forum on social issues—in addition to six different adult study groups scattered through the week including a men's breakfast on Friday morning, a two-and-one-half-hour Bible study group on Tuesday evening, and a women's Bible study group on Thursday afternoons. This contrasts with the traditional Sunday morning adult program that is organized by age and/or marital status.

How much variety do you offer people in the group life of your congregation?

How Old Are the Groups?

Most face-to-face groups that have been meeting on a weekly basis for more than a few months tend to become exclusionary. Most groups that have been together for an extended period of time tend to want new members, but often are perceived as closed and exclusionary by potential new members. The biggest single exception to that generalization are the groups organized around a purpose or goal that is easier to fulfill or attain if the group has more members. Examples include the group responsible for the big money-raising-for-missions dinner scheduled for October, the adult choir, the men's group that takes the complete responsibility for care of the building, the group that is organized to make once-a-year caring calls on each member, and the group that is organized to sponsor a new mission. By contrast, most groups organized for study or fellowship or mutual support tend to become exclusionary very quickly.

Out of that context comes the basic rule of "new groups for new people." It also explains why many staff persons responsible for the group life of a congregation concentrate more of their time and energy on helping to give birth to the new rather than on trying to keep dying groups alive. That set of priorities, however, will not be popular with every member!

Living with Pluralism

There are many reasons why the group life is critical to the health and vitality of middle-sized congregations, but three deserve special emphasis. Perhaps the most widely recognized today is the critical importance of the group life in the assimilation of new members.[1] A second is the nurture of members. A third, which sometimes is overlooked, is that homogeneous face-to-face groups help the pluralistic congregation survive many internal conflicts and those choosing-up-of-sides episodes that otherwise might be highly disruptive.

The most controversial thesis to come out of the church growth movement is that most numerically growing congregations attract and include new members who closely resemble the present members. The homogeneous unit principle is an accurate reflection of reality. The one exception to that generalization is that some pluralistic congregations are experiencing substantial numerical growth. They are able to be exceptions to the homogeneous unit principle because of a strong emphasis on an extensive network of homogeneous face-to-face groups. The vast majority of the numerically growing pluralistic churches also benefit from the guidance of a leader (usually a minister and often the senior pastor) who is skilled in the management of a highly pluralistic organization. An outstanding example of this combination of pluralism and numerical growth has been The Central Presbyterian Church of Richland, Washington.

Does your congregation look to the group life as a means of minimizing some of the tensions that are an inevitable product of pluralism?

Gluing the Group Together

"Our problem is that our nine-year-old daughter doesn't like it here," explained the thirty-five-year-old Brenda Gray who had been born and reared in First Church. "We live nearly five miles north of here and we're in a different school district than most of the members. My husband and I met while we were in college and we lived in another part of the country for ten years after we were married. When we moved here two years ago, I naturally wanted to come back here to church. I was a little disappointed to find that most of my old friends were gone, but my husband and I really do like it here. We only wish our daughter could find some friends. I wish they would plan a slumber party for the girls in that fourth-grade Sunday school class. That would be a way of helping her meet and make new friends."

"Perhaps the most unusual group here is the Century Club," commented the Sunday school superintendent at the Hilltop Church. "It began as an adult Sunday school class back in the early fifties. The entrance requirement was that the combined ages of the husband and wife had to be at least one hundred years. For a good many years it was the strongest class in the church, and many of our most influential leaders came out of that class. From the very beginning the members developed the tradition of a big social evening on the third Saturday of every month. They eat together, sing, tell stories, and play games. For several years that event also served as an entry point for new members to join the class. About three years ago, when we remodeled the building, the class was forced out of its room and the members decided not to meet on Sunday morning until after the remodeling had been completed and they could return to their room. Well, to make a long story short, the remodeling took more than a year and during that time their teacher retired and moved to New Mexico. When the time came for them to resume their Sunday morning classes, they decided they weren't interested and told us we could use their old room for a new class. We did need the space and accepted their offer. They continue to meet for a social event every month, but none of them attend an adult class. They still refer to themselves as an adult class, but they never meet on Sunday morning!"

"Last year we kept a careful record of the attendance of the fifth and sixth grade class," explained the superintendent of the church school at Community Church. "That's the only class that has a party every month. It also is our biggest class. We found that the attendance for the Sunday morning following the party on Friday evening or Saturday was the peak for that month. The typical pattern was twenty-eight or twenty-nine or thirty the Sunday right after the party. It then generally declined until there were about twenty-two or twenty-three in attendance on the Sunday before the party. The kids come from several different school districts and the class is taught by a team of three teachers. I suggested to the teacher the parties were a means of gluing the class back together again."

These three stories illustrate some of the issues that may be encountered when a congregation seeks to strengthen its group life.

During the past thirty-five years some remarkably revealing research has been carried out on how a gathering of strangers can be turned into a closely knit, cohesive, and supportive unit. The issues at which this research has been directed range from the extensive use of drugs by students in large high schools to the low morale of the enlisted men in the American army in Vietnam to the growth of the women's liberation movement to how large a team's roster should be in the National Football League to the decline of voluntarism in our society to the growth of the nondenominational churches during past three decades to the rapid growth of parachurch youth groups to the common characteristics of the strongest Sunday school classes.

Out of this research have come scores of insights that have proved to be useful in strengthening the cohesiveness among the members of a group. Before looking at several of these, it must be noted that most include "trade offs." In other words, to gain one particular advantage, usually something else has to be sacrificed. Most of us cannot continue to eat ice cream and also lose weight. That is a trade off. Another trade off is that the stronger the sense of cohesion and unity in a group, the more likely that group will tend to be seen as exclusionary by newcomers.

Much of this research on small unit cohesion can be summarized in ten guidelines that can be used in your congregation to strengthen the group life.

1. Live Together Overnight

The slumber party for the girls in the fourth-grade Sunday school, the weekend retreat for members of the Men's Fellowship, the overnight camping trip for the members of that newly formed young couples Sunday school class, the ski trip weekend by the high school youth group, the overnight visit to a theological seminary by members of the governing board, the three-day-two-night visit to a home mission project by the members of the eighth-grade confirmation class, the six-day choir trip by the youth choir, the weekend attendance at a church growth workshop by members of the evangelism committee, and the fifth-grade Sunday school class going to church camp for a week in July are examples of this approach of reinforcing cohesion in a group.

2. Begin the New Venture Together

Most of us prefer to help pioneer something new, rather than feel like a "Johnny-come-lately" joining a long established group. A common application of this guideline is the admonition to start new groups to help assimilate new members.

3. Encourage Continuity in Leadership

Changing leaders or teachers frequently is one means of undermining unit cohesion. This is one of several arguments in support of long pastorates, for encouraging Sunday school teachers to teach the same group for several years, and for building in continuity in the adult leadership of youth groups—and, as the U. S. Army discovered in Vietnam, for not changing company commanders every six months. Rotation in office for administrative leaders has more merit than rotation in office for program leaders.

4. Participate in a Shared-Work Experience

The widespread application of this guideline in the churches is illustrated by the bazaar conducted by members of the women's organization, the annual car wash by the high school youth, the door-to-door religious census conducted by members of the evangelism committee, the singing of the Messiah by the chancel choir, the pancake breakfast served by the Men's Fellowship, the spring cleanup of the church property, the annual cookie sale by the Girl Scouts, the repainting of the sanctuary by that adult Sunday school class, the presentation of *Jesus Christ Superstar* by the youth fellowship, and the mission work tour.

5. Share in a Structured Study Experience

This approach to building a sense of cohesion and unity is illustrated by the Bethel Bible Study program, by the parenting classes, by the study trip to the Holy Land, by the high school Bible study group, by the twenty-week new member orientation class for adults, by the confirmation class for youth, by the study groups in the women's organization, and by the research program of the long-range planning committee.

6. Pioneer New Goals

This approach can be illustrated by the sense of unity among the charter members of a new church, by the close friendship ties of that group who launched a new men's fellowship, by the persons who are now participating in their sixth consecutive church camping weekend that was initiated a few years ago, by the members of the committee that planned the new building, by the group that started the first handbell choir, by the folks who organized the Wednesday after-school educational program for children, or by the pioneers who initiated the adding of that Saturday evening worship service to the schedule.

7. Meet in the Same Place

The importance of a familiar place in people's lives may be the most neglected item on this list. Group cohesion is reinforced by meeting in the same physical setting whenever possible. That generalization applies to the first-grade Sunday school class, the weekend camping experience, the adult choir rehearsal, the monthly meeting of the governing board, and staff meetings in the large church.

8. Grow Old Together

There is a natural tendency among human beings to stay with the same persons or groups. The "rotation" or "promotion" principle used in most Sunday schools, in many women's organizations, and in other groups in the churches runs counter to this. In some churches this principle is followed in encouraging continued membership in the same circle in the women's organization, in making this year's third- and fourth-grade Sunday school class into next year's fourth- and fifth-grade Sunday school class, and in encouraging adults to continue in the same class year after year.

9. Identify a Common Enemy

This is the oldest organizing principle on this list and was the heart of the Prohibition movement in the first quarter of this century. Today it is used to develop a sense of cohesiveness in the group combating world hunger or seeking reforms in infant nutrition or in promoting biblical inerrancy or in reinforcing the dikes with sandbags during the spring flood or in organizing weight reduction clubs or in building support for the hostages or in increasing the budget of the Department of Defense.

10. Plan Friendship Building Events

This approach was illustrated by the Century Club at the Hilltop Church and is widely used by tens of thousands of churches. The seven common characteristics of these events are: (1) food, (2) music, (3) humor and laughter, (4) informal fellowship, (5) a structure or schedule that provides a sense of movement or progression to the event, (6) a dependable and regularly scheduled meeting date and time, and (7) perhaps most critical of all, a leader or a leadership team that accepts the responsibility for planning and overseeing this type of event.

Frequently three or four or five of these guidelines are combined in a single experience.

Which of these guidelines can be used to strengthen the cohesiveness of that second-grade Sunday school class that includes children from several school districts? Which can be used to reinforce the cohesiveness of other groups? Which ones are consistent with your values and goals?

Who Is in Charge?

The fifth area of concern in reviewing the group life in your congregation is based on a simple, but critical, question. Who is responsible for the general oversight, care, and nurture of the group life in your congregation? Who is responsible for counseling groups in need of revitalization? Who is responsible for maintaining the health of existing groups? Who will take the initiative to organize new groups in response to the changing needs of people? Who makes sure that loyal leaders and workers are recognized and thanked? Who will help newcomers find a home in one of the groups in your congregation? Who will repeatedly affirm the value and importance of each group to the members of that group as well as to others? Who will help each group see the need for an occasional "regluing" of group ties? Who is in charge of the group life in your congregation?

Where Are We Represented?

The final self-appraisal on group life lifts up one of the basic differences between small membership congregations and the big churches. In the typical small membership church the members of each class or group feel it is important that their group be represented on the governing board of that church. "We want a member of our group to be a policy maker here" is the basic issue.

By contrast, in many large congregations the members of a particular group typically are much more concerned that they be represented on the program staff. "Who represents our group and our interests at staff meetings?" is the central issue in the large congregation. Representation on the governing board usually is perceived as a minor concern. These members recognize that in most large churches most of the critical decisions on direction, priorities, schedules, and program development are made by the staff. This is an especially significant issue in the highly pluralistic congregation. Each segment of that pluralistic church wants to be sure its interests are represented in staff meetings.

What is the basic principle for the representation of the groups in your congregation? Is that the appropriate principle for a congregation of this size, type, and role?

11

How Do You Conceptualize Programming?

"In the long run you must plan to house the three basic functions every church is engaged in—worship, education, and fellowship," explained the architect to the building planning committee of the two-year-old Anchor Park Church. "In this design I am suggesting that for your first unit you construct one large room that can serve as the setting for corporate worship for several years. Eventually it can become your permanent fellowship hall. In addition, this first unit will include four classrooms, an office for the pastor, a small kitchen, and restrooms."

"We have nine standing committees here at First Church," explained one of the long-time members to the orientation class for new members, "Christian education, worship, finance, evangelism, social concerns, missions, membership, personnel, and the trustees. Some people do not consider the trustees to be a committee since they have their own treasury, but they really are the equivalent of a standing committee. Every bit of business that comes up here at First Church is channeled through one of those nine committees."

"We're a thirteen-hundred-member church and we have forty-five people in the chancel choir on the average Sunday," complained the senior minister at Trinity Church. "Zion Church has only six hundred members and I'm told they have between thirty-five and forty in their chancel choir every Sunday. If we're twice as big, it seems to me we should have twice as many people in our choir."

These three comments illustrate one of the most neglected questions that should be asked in the self-appraisal process. What is the conceptual framework you use for defining the program and ministry of your congregation and for creating the organizational structure?

One response to that question is that the vast majority of church buildings on this continent have been designed around the trinity of worship, education, and fellowship. Another conceptual framework is reflected in the system of functional committees (finance, worship, education, missions) that have been created to oversee the operation of a parish. A third response is to think in terms of choirs rather than in terms of a ministry of music. Another example of this conceptual framework is illustrated in the titles given to staff members in large congregations such as senior minister, director of Christian education, membership secretary, youth minister, choir director, and minister of visitation.

In other words, the usual response is to develop a conceptual framework that reflects the job that needs to be done. We need a choir so we find a choir director. Our central reason for being is the corporate worship of God so we need a place to gather and someone to lead us in worship and to preach the Word. We need to pass the Word on to our children, so we need rooms for Sunday school classes, a committee to oversee the educational ministry, and perhaps a staff person to direct the program.

What Are the Alternatives?

The central thesis of this chapter is that the conceptual framework used to identify both the needs, and the responses to needs, will have a profound influence on the content of that programmatic response, on the participation by lay volunteers, on the role and responsibilities of paid staff, on the organizational structure of the congregation, on the allocation of scarce resources such as time, money, space, energy, and talents, on the weekly schedule, and on the evangelistic outreach of a congregation. If that thesis can be demonstrated, it means this is a very important issue for the self-appraisal committee.

There are many alternative approaches and this can be illustrated by looking at four different areas of ministry. In each case the example used raises questions about values and goals, as well as about that particular area of ministry. The self-appraisal committee will want to consider values and goals as they look at these suggestions for a different conceptual framework.

Choirs or Ministry of Music?

"We have an adult choir, a youth choir, and a children's choir," explained the choir director in a three-hundred-member congregation. "That means every family who joins this church can find a choir for each member of the family if they're interested."

When asked about the content of the music program at the nine-hundred-member Central Church, the minister of music replied, "That's a complicated question. The music program here does not exist in a vacuum by itself. We see it as a part of worship, of the educational program, of the fellowship life, and especially as an entry point for new members to become involved in life at Central. We have fourteen continuing organized music groups. These include the chancel choir that sings at our eleven o'clock service, a men and boy's choir that sings twice a month at the eight-thirty service, a high school youth choir, a junior high choir, three different children's choirs, four handbell groups, an orchestra, brass ensemble, and a community chorus that includes a lot of non-members and sings for about two dozen programs in the general community during the course of a year. In addition, we have four trained volunteers who circulate among the classes in the children's division of the Sunday school every week. Each one spends about five to ten minutes in a class leading the singing and teaching new songs. These four volunteers cover all sixteen classes every week. We also have 'dinner at the theater' every spring. That includes dessert followed by the play on Friday night and a full dinner followed by the same play on Saturday night. These are held in our fellowship hall and we serve about seven hundred people in the two evenings. That's usually a fun type of play. Last year we did a Charlie Brown play, and half of the people who constituted the cast and the crew were persons who had joined Central during the previous twelve months. In the fall we do a serious religious drama and we usually offer that over two consecutive weekends. Once a year our high school youth group puts on a musical; the first of these, of course, was *Godspell*. We also have a part in the Missions Festival every fall and, of course, music is a big part of the hanging of the greens program in Advent, at Christmas, during Lent, and for each of our large group fellowship events that we schedule about nine or ten times a year here at Central."

These two descriptive statements illustrate one difference between thinking in terms of choirs and using a conceptual framework that opens the door to a larger and broader music program. In general, you get what you plan for in programming.

A second difference is that the usual approach, "We have to have a choir as a part of Sunday morning service," usually means that no more than 10 to 15 percent of the members will be active participants—except in the large churches where that approach often means no more than 5 to 10 percent of the members will be active participants in the choir program.

By contrast an extensive ministry of music often will involve 30 to 60 percent of the membership. In general, the more extensive the program, the wider the range of gifts and talents that are needed and appreciated.

Overlapping that is a third issue. Why do chancel choirs rarely include more than thirty to fifty voices, regardless of the size of the congregation? One response is that most choirs are organized around either small group or middle-sized group dynamics and that influences the number of participants. If the goal is to involve more people, one alternative is to organize the chancel choir using large group organizational principles. A more common response is to increase participation by creating a larger number and a greater variety of vocal groups.

Finally, the Central Church approach illustrates how music can supplement, support, and reinforce a variety of programs and ministries and that brings up the second of these four questions on your conceptual framework for programming.

Compete or Reinforce?

"More than half of our adult choir members never join a Sunday school class because that would mean walking out of the class every Sunday about fifteen minutes before the class adjourns in order to robe and warm up with the choir," explained the Sunday school superintendent in one congregation.

"The biggest source of conflict I have to put up with is the constant battle between our Sunday school teachers and the weekday nursery school that uses those same rooms during the week," complained the pastor of an inner-city church.

These two comments illustrate a common problem. One program is seen as competing with another for people's time and/or for space and/or resources. This is a natural, normal, and predictable phenomenon. Some will attribute it to "empire building" while others will relate it to the doctrine of original sin. It is a normal product of institutional pressures. One response is to treat it as an inevitable consequence of a multifaceted program and plead with everyone to be patient and tolerant.

A better response is to change the conceptual framework. Instead of concentrating on the individual components, look at the larger picture in order to determine what can be done to make one ministry strengthen and reinforce the other.

One example of that is the ministry of music at Central Church which is designed to supplement and strengthen the Sunday school classes in the children's division, the fellowship life of that parish, the missions program, the assimilation of new members, the ministry with youth, and the large group life of that congregation as well as corporate worship.

Another example is the church that inserted a twenty-five minute coffee break between the end of the Sunday school period and the call to worship. A third illustration is the church that created a seven-day-a-week Early Childhood Development Center that includes both the Sunday school classes for children, the weekday nursery (which offers a schedule of Sunday-Tuesday-Thursday sessions for three-year-olds and a Sunday-Monday-Wednesday-Friday schedule for four-year-olds with the same adults in that room for the three-day schedule for three-year-olds and the same adults in the room for the four-day schedule for four-year-olds). The Early Childhood Development Center also sponsors parenting classes, a Sunday school class for parents of young children, a circle in the women's organization for mothers of children in the weekday nursery, occasional classes for new step-parents, and a support group for single parents. A fourth example is the church that makes both stewardship education and the educational component of the missions program a part of the ministry of education. Another example is the church that created a youth council to oversee and coordinate all ministries involving the teen-agers.

Does your organizational structure and conceptual framework encourage various pograms to compete for people's time and for priorities on resources or are they designed to complement and reinforce one another?

Individuals or Families?

"We're a family-oriented parish and our primary focus is on reaching and serving families," declared one of the most influential leaders at Calvary Church. "Our staff includes a part-time youth director, a part-time educational assistant, a part-time children's worker, and a part-time minister of visitation as well as our pastor who is full-time."

That represents a very common approach to staffing the self-identified family-centered church. It is based on a very clear and easy-to-understand assumption, "We have a job to do and we will need some additional specialized staff to help do that job."

A radically different approach begins with a different conceptual framework. "We're a family-centered church and we see four different types of family settings we need to reach and serve. One is the young childless couples, and they represent a rapidly growing proportion of all families. A second is families that include young children. A third is families that include teen-agers, and of course many families fit both of these categories. The fourth is the growing number of empty nesters. Therefore we have a part-time staff person to work with young childless couples, a part-time staff person specializing in ministries with families that include young children, a part-time staffer who works with families that include teen-agers, and a part-time person who specializes in ministries with middle-aged and older adults. Perhaps our most interesting program that has emerged from this approach is our POT group; it is a mutual support group for parents of teen-agers."

In program development in your church do you think in terms of individuals or family settings?

Director of What?

In the years following the close of World War II thousands of Protestant congregations, for the first time in their history, added a second professional to the program staff. Sometimes that second person was an associate minister, but frequently the new position carried the title, director of Christian education. A few years later many congregations created another position which usually carried the title youth director or youth minister. The sixties saw many urban churches create a new program staff position, the director of community ministries.

These increases in program staff were a natural consequence of (a) the increasing emphasis on specialists, (b) the "religious revival" of the fifties, (c) a more affluent society that enables us to hire someone to do that which formerly was done by volunteers, (d) the expanding expectations placed on the churches, (e) the urbanization of society, (f) the hunger for better educational programs throughout our culture, (g) the availability of academically trained specialists and a dozen other factors.

In the sixties this trend came to a fork in the road and took a new direction, especially in the southeastern section of the United States. Scores of churches began to take a second look at their program and came out with a new conceptual framework. Instead of thinking in terms of the traditional trinity of worship, education, and fellowship, the leaders of these congregations recognized (a) their program had grown and was now both varied and complex, (b) the expansion of the worship schedule to include two or three or four or five corporate worship experiences every weekend had greatly increased the work load on the pastor and thus reduced the time and energy that person had left to oversee the expanding program, (c) the conflicts in the schedule and the competition among the various programs now exceeded the capability of the governing board to mediate the resulting tensions, and (d) the frustration level was rising among the lay volunteers because no one had a good answer to the question, Who is in charge around here?

One result was the creation of the position of program director or minister of program in hundreds and hundreds of mansions, ranches, and nations. The creation of this position reflects a sharply different conceptual framework from the traditional approach in which each of six or eight different program committees was a miniature church with its own specialized staff person.

These examples are offered to illustrate the thesis that the conceptual framework you use in your congregation for looking at ministry and program will influence the design and use of the meeting house, the roles, responsibilities, and titles of paid staff members, the organizational structure you need in your parish, the content of the program, the priorities that will influence the schedule and the allocation of scarce resources, the breadth of participation of lay volunteers, the capability of a congregation to reach, attract, and assimilate new members, the willingness to venture into new ministries and new programs, and the frustration level of both staff and lay volunteers.

What is the conceptual framework you use in looking at the ministry and program of your congregation? Do all of the leaders use the same approach? Is it the appropriate approach for a congregation of this size and type? For a church with this purpose and role? (The conceptual framework that may be appropriate in one church may be counterproductive if imported into another congregation!) Has it changed since the present pastor arrived on the scene? Should it? Are staff roles and responsibilities consistent with the current conceptual framework? Does anyone really care?

12

WHAT ARE OUR ASSUMPTIONS
ABOUT YOUTH MINISTRIES?

"I have a two-part approach to youth ministries," explained the twenty-six-year-old associate minister who was near the end of his second year on the staff at First Church. "Sunday morning, I believe, should focus on serious study. That's the time for teen-agers to study the Bible, to learn the teachings of the Christian faith, and to gain an understanding of the history of the church. Sunday evenings can be spent on fellowship, on putting into practice the way Christians relate to one another, and on building the group identity of the youth fellowship."

"I understand you have nearly seventy high school youth in this congregation. What proportion of them participate in Sunday school and in the Sunday evening fellowship?" inquired a visitor.

"Well, to tell you the truth, attendance in the Sunday morning class averages only about twelve to fifteen," admitted the associate minister, "and our Sunday evening group usually attracts between fifteen and twenty. High school kids are awfully busy in this community and there is a lot of competition for their time. Nearly half of them have part-time jobs and a lot of them have to work Sunday evenings. It's hard today to interest the kids in church."

This brief conversation lifts up a series of questions that merit discussion in any church seeking to review its ministries with youth.[1] Several of these reflect the difference in perspective between the youth and the adults who are responsible for the oversight of the program.

Cafeteria or Five-Course Meal?

"You might compare our approach to youth ministries to a five-course meal," explained the fifty-three-year-old layperson at Trinity Church who chaired the youth council. "We offer our high school age youth a five-part package consisting of a Sunday school class, worship, a youth choir, a Tuesday evening youth fellowship, and the quarterly district rallies in which we join with a dozen other churches on the afternoon of the fifth Sunday. The reason I compare it with a five-course meal is we expect every one of our youth to partake of each of the five courses. If you skip two or three of the components of a five-course meal, you will be nutritionally deprived. We believe that any teen-ager who skips one or more of the components of our youth program will be spiritually deprived. I have to admit, however, that less than one-half of our kids participate in as many as three of the programs I just described to you."

"Imagine that I am holding a basket in my hands and this basket contains all the programs, events, ministries, and opportunities for meaningful involvement that are open to high school youth in this congregation," explained the visitor who was interviewing a dozen high school students who were active in the youth program at North Church. "Obviously your Sunday morning church school class is one and the Sunday evening youth group is a second. What are the others?"

"The youth choir," offered a sixteen-year-old girl.

"Retreats in the spring and fall," added a seventeen-year-old boy.

Within five minutes the group had identified seventeen different components of the total youth program at North Church. The list included Sunday school, the youth fellowship, the youth choir, weekend retreats every fall and spring, money-raising activities, parties, ushering, the summer work-camp experience at a denominational mission post, the six-day youth choir trip during spring vacation, the summer camping experience at the denominational church camp, the three-times-a-year youth rallies sponsored by the regional judicatory of that denomination, summer recreational events such as swimming parties and volleyball games, helping teach in the vacation Bible school, the Bible study group that met for an hour early on Tuesday mornings during Lent, the winter ski trip that was a cooperative venture involving North Church and two neighboring congregations, the booth that the youth planned and staffed at the mission festival sponsored every October by the missions committee at North Church, and the chance to tutor younger children in the nearby elementary school that had been "adopted" by North Church as its neighborhood mission effort.

While North Church has a more extensive youth program than most congregations, these comments illustrate a basic point in the evaluation of youth ministries. Frequently the youth see the youth program as a cafeteria while the adults think of it as a four- or five- or six-course meal. Furthermore, the teen-agers usually perceive the program to be far more extensive than do most of the adults. If asked to name the components of the youth program at North Church, few of the adults would list more than four or five or six of the various components.

What are the components of the youth program in your congregation? Is it perceived as a five-course meal or as a cafeteria? Who is best equipped to answer that question? Are the leaders aware of the full range of events, experiences, and opportunities that constitute the youth program in your church?

What Is the Participation Rate?

After the teen-agers of North Church had identified these seventeen different components of the total youth program, the various activities and events were listed on a sheet of newsprint. It should be noted at this point that forty-six of the 577 confirmed members of North Church were in grades nine through twelve at the local four-year high school. That figures out to be 8 percent and 8 percent of all Americans age fourteen and over are in that four-year age bracket.

"Approximately how many of the forty-six youth in this church participate in each of these programs?" inquired the outsider.

"That's hard to answer the way you ask it," replied one of the teen-agers. "You see, we invite other kids who aren't from this church to come to some of our things. Our program isn't limited just to our own kids."

"There are about ten or fifteen of that forty-six we never see," explained a seventeen-year-old, "but during the course of the year we'll have at least that many youth who are not members here to share with us in some of these activities. So I suppose you could say that our potential for any one event is between forty-five and fifty."

"Yeah, but we've never had anywhere close to that," interjected another teen-ager. "Even at our parties we never have more than thirty. The only time we ever have more than thirty is when we do something that involves other churches such as our ski trip or the district youth rallies."

A half hour later, after reviewing membership lists, these teen-agers at North Church agreed that the largest participation was in the various parties and recreational events. Between twenty-five and thirty of the forty-six teen-agers from North Church attended some of these events. Only three were involved on a regular basis as tutors at the nearby elementary school, twenty-one, including four non-members, had gone on the work-camp trip to Appalachia the previous summer, seventeen were regular members of the youth choir, and eighteen to twenty attended the Sunday school class.

When these dozen teen-agers were asked about their own participation in the seventeen different programs and activities, two said they were involved in fifteen of the seventeen, one in thirteen, two in twelve, one in eleven, one in ten, two in nine, one in eight, one in six, and one said that in the course of a year he might be involved in five of the seventeen on that list.

There are several generalizations on participation that can be illustrated by the youth program at North Church. First, the larger the number of teen-agers in the congregation, the smaller the proportion who regularly participate in the youth program. Second, in the larger churches several of the teen-agers, frequently as many as one-third to one-half, will not participate in any aspect of the youth program. Third, one by-product of the large consolidated high school is that today's teenagers have learned (a) the world offers them a huge array of choices, (b) they cannot say yes to all of the choices, (c) they have learned how to be selective and experienced at responding "count me out," and (d) they do not feel guilty about saying, "No, that's not for me."

Fourth, in most churches with a moderate size program only a minority of the youth will be involved in as many as one-half of the events and activities. Fifth, the youth of today do have many pressures on their schedules. While the academic demands of the high school may have declined for many, special honors programs, sports, extracurricular activities and, for many, time on the school bus do eat up several hours of the week. In thousands of public systems a majority of the sixteen-, seventeen-, and eighteen-year-olds have part-time jobs during the school year that require fifteen to thirty hours a week. That is one of the greatest changes in our culture since 1970 and has had a tremendous impact on youth ministries.

The participation rate is a result of an assortment of several factors, one of which is the goals of the youth program. That raises what may be the most important single question in reviewing the ministry with youth.

What Are Your Goals and What Is Your Approach?

"I believe our top priority for next year should be to hire someone to strengthen our ministry to youth," said a church council member. "After all, the youth of today will make up the church of tomorrow."

"It seems to me that we should expect parents to take a greater interest in our youth program," said another. "If parents refuse to serve as counselors, how can they expect anyone else to do it."

"I can remember when I was a teen-ager and we had a great youth program in this church," said a third. "We must have had at least thirty kids in the youth choir singing twice a month. That choir and our director made our youth program go. If we could get a good choir director, we could build our program back up."

Those comments represent a widespread anxiety point in churches today. How can we strengthen our youth ministry? How can we attract more of our young people? What can we do to rebuild our youth program?

These three comments also illustrate the diversity of opinion on the philosophy and goals of a ministry to youth. The first reflected a belief that the best approach would be to hire a youth director. The second declared that the leadership for the youth ministry should be drawn from parents. The third expressed a conviction that music and a good youth choir would be most effective.

It would be easy to move next into a debate about which of these alternative courses of action is the best approach for that congregation. It may be better, however, to raise other questions. First, where do we begin? Why do we want to encourage a special church program for teen-agers?

Are we looking for large numbers? Or are we primarily concerned about the spiritual and personal growth of our young people? Are we more concerned about a program for children from member families or about reaching youth not actively involved in the life of any congregation? Is the number-one objective to teach the Bible? Are we trying to encourage a relationship between each teen-ager and the church that will continue through adulthood? Do we want to prepare the youth for that eventual move that will take many of them out of their home church and make it easier for them to find a new church home? Are we trying to instill a loyalty to this congregation or to this denominational family? Is our primary goal to help each young person discover what it means to lead a Christian life and to live according to the teachings of Jesus Christ? Are we spending this time, energy, and money in the hope of rearing replacement leaders and members for our congregation?

While it is tempting to respond "all of the above," that is being evasive. To plan effectively for youth ministry, a number one goal is essential. The other "hopes" are secondary or supportive.

Having set that goal, we need to determine whether it is consistent with the approach used in carrying out the program. Perhaps the best way to explain this point is to review a list of different approaches to youth ministry found in churches today.

A widely used approach is to "farm it out" to a bright young staff member such as a college student, seminary intern, associate minister, youth director, or the newly arrived young pastor and hope that a magnetic personality will attract a swarm of youth like a candle attracts bugs in the summer. When that candle dims or burns out, we replace it with a new and more attractive candle to attract a new swarm. This approach provides a relatively passive and non-challenging role for adults.

A more common approach is to expect the parents "who created the problem" to take care of it by volunteering as counselors and teachers in the youth program.

Since some young people resist the idea of involvement of parents and other adults from their parents' generation, a widely used alternative is to recruit husband-wife teams in their twenties or early thirties, who are "Young enough to keep up with the kids" and too young to remind youth of parents. Frequently a program built around fellowship, recreation, special events, and serious studies results. But no one is sure which of these four components is the program's top priority.

A growing number of churches recruit and train eight to twelve adults to serve as a closely knit counseling team. The team is present at each youth meeting and most, if not all, members accompany the youth on trips or to a special event. This approach is based on the premise that the most important goal of a youth program is to expose each youth to a variety of models of adult Christians.

A common approach is to build the program around a choir or a music-drama model. This approach capitalizes on music as both a unifying force and an opportunity for creative individual participation. This program is usually staffed by a paid person and/or volunteer adult leaders. Frequently it includes one or more major choir trips each year as well as a concert and/or the presentation of a religious drama—each of these serves as a unifying rallying point.

A modest proportion of churches have followed the covenant model in which the youth covenant with one another on expectations, discipline, participation, and goals. This usually is built around the youth director or the youth minister as the central figure and may be dependent on the continued presence of that person.

A growing approach to youth ministries is to build the program around a service or outreach emphasis modeled on the commandment to love your neighbor. This approach emphasizes helping youth identify their special gifts and using these gifts in service to others.

Some middle-sized and large congregations build the program around a series of events, experiences, trips, and service projects with a systematic emphasis on participatory learning events. In several of these congregations the "youth room" is a reconditioned bus.

Many congregations have built their program around Bible study. This group, which may include twenty-five to sixty teen-agers, meets weekly for two to three hours to study what the Bible says to their concerns. It is common for a majority of the participants to come from non-member homes and less than a fourth of the young people from member families.

A distinctive approach to youth ministry is based on the premise that the purpose for a program is to help each young person develop greater self-awareness and a stronger self-image. This may be accomplished through group experiences, workshops in interpersonal communication, and helping each young person acquire a new competence or skill (such as leading a discussion group, playing a musical instrument, participating in a Bible study or outreach program, or planning and leading a corporate worship experience).

Many youth programs aim at developing a positive attitude toward the church so that young people will have happy church memories. This approach usually emphasizes games, recreational events, and social gatherings.

Some churches have concluded that the reason for a youth program is to secure a permanent and lifetime commitment to Christ from each young person. Frequently this approach includes a Bible study emphasis, personal testimonies, exhortation, camping experiences, and articulate adult models of Christians.

A growing number of congregations have built their confirmation and/or youth program around three words: service, study, and sacrifice. Each youth is expected to be an active participant in a project serving others, to be engaged in serious study of the Bible and the Christian faith, and to be challenged to sacrifice.

A few congregations have changed their organizational structure in an attempt to prevent the "dropping out of church" of eighteen-, nineteen-, and twenty-year-olds. One approach that has had interesting results is to form a group of junior high age youth. Instead of annually "promoting" one grade out and a new grade in, the group remains together. Each year the age boundaries are raised twelve months. The first year it is for seventh, eighth, and ninth graders. The second year, that same group becomes a fellowship of eighth, ninth, and tenth graders. Six or seven years later, what began as a collection of thirteen-, fourteen-, and fifteen-year-olds has become a larger and more cohesive group of nineteen- to twenty-three-year-olds. The process of "growing old together" has welded a closely knit group that attracts newcomers.

Several years ago an approach emerged to integrate youth into the adult-oriented congregational programs, committees, activities, and responsibilities. This approach was based on the assumption that confirmed teen-agers were full members of that parish with the same rights and responsibilities as adults and should be treated as adults. Experience with this approach has demonstrated that the elimination of special groups, programs, and activities directed at teen-agers usually has been paralleled by a decrease in the number of young people in that congregation.

One approach used by several large churches offers a three-, four-, or five-track program. One staff member is responsible for the youth choir and drama group. A dozen lay volunteers are responsible for a second track (or activity) for another group of youth. A paid staff member and four or five lay volunteers are responsible for a third track and another staff member is responsible for developing a fourth track. The expectation is that few teen-agers will participate in more than one of these tracks. Since each young person has a range of activity choices offered him or her by the public schools, the church also offers a range of choices.

Finally, a number of congregations have adopted the local operation of one of the parachurch youth movements, such as Young Life, Campus Crusade, or Youth for Christ. The adults in these churches urge teen-agers to become a part of one of these parachurch groups, which usually is staffed by a person selected by that parachurch, rather than by the congregational leaders. Sometimes that parish houses meetings of one of these groups, and members of other churches see it as "their" program.

This is not an exhaustive list of approaches used by churches today in youth ministries. It would be easy to lengthen the list with the covenant-caring community, the religious drama group, the individual counseling approach, or another dozen approaches. That is not the point. The list simply illustrates the variety of ideas being used and suggests that the choice of an approach is important in setting a youth ministry goal. What approach are you following in your church today?

A final consideration is available resources. What will be needed to start the approach we have chosen to accomplish our basic purpose? What do we need for adult staff? For a meeting place? For curriculum and similar resources? For in-service training for adults?

These questions should be asked *after* a goal and approach have been chosen. Too often, however, we see parish leaders deciding to hire a youth director, call a youth minister or recruit volunteer leadership for the youth program without giving any serious thought to the purpose behind the existence of a special program for teen-agers or evaluation of alternatives. Until these decisions have been made, it is premature to begin mobilizing resources or assigning responsibilities. The path selected and the resources assembled should be consistent with the basic direction chosen.

Until that has been done, it also will be difficult to make an evaluation of either the youth program or of the adult leadership for that important specialized ministry.

What Are the Components of a Strong Program?

The place is a midwestern city of eighteen thousand residents. The month is April. You are sitting by yourself in the corner listening to an outsider interview three members from eighty-five-year-old Trinity Church.

The outsider is a leader from a congregation in another county who came to discover how Trinity Church has developed such a strong handbell choir with high school youth. The outsider is talking with (1) a seventeen-year-old member of the youth handbell choir, (2) the director of the handbell choir, and (3) the forty-two-year-old parent of a fifteen-year-old girl who is a loyal member of this bell choir.

Your assignment is to listen to this conversation and identify the general characteristics of the program that have helped produce such a closely knit youth group. In other words, what are they doing at Trinity Church that you might consider introducing into the organization and operation of the youth ministry in your parish?

Outsider: How many young people are in your handbell choir?

Teen-ager: There are twenty-one of us. We're all tenth-, eleventh-, and twelth-graders, but because the town is in the northeastern corner of the county, the kids come from three different high schools.

Parent: Let me add it's a very loyal and dedicated group! They're great kids. They never miss a rehearsal and they're really a closely knit group of young people.

Outsider: You mean every one of these teen-agers attends every rehearsal? That's hard to believe today with all the pressures on high school kids for their time. How do you pull that off?

Choir Director: That's easy. That's a part of the covenant. When they sign up to be in the handbell choir, they commit themselves to attend every rehearsal, every service at which the bell choir plays and also to attend bell choir camp for a week in June. If they aren't willing to make that commitment, they can't be members.

Outsider: You mean everyone goes to bell choir camp every June? How many are going this June?

Teen-ager: Twenty-one!

Choir Director: No, that's not quite right. Only twenty are going this June.

Outsider: What happened to that twenty-first member?

Director: She can't go with us because she won a scholarship to a midwestern regional handbell choir camp and that is held the same week as our state camp.

Outsider: How much does it cost to go to the state camp? Who pays for that?

Parent: This year it will cost approximately $7,400 for transportation, tuition, meals, housing, and a side trip of three days of sightseeing for the twenty kids and four adults. We raise it through a series of dinners. This year we've had five dinners and we have one to go. Each dinner usually produces a profit of approximately $1,300 to $1,600. We had bad weather for our February dinner, so we have to raise at least $1,800 at our dinner next month if we're going to make it. We don't get a nickel out of the church budget. We pay our own way! The handbells were purchased as a memorial and given to the church, but except for the bells we pay for everything.

Director: That's not quite accurate. The church does pay me a salary of three hundred dollars a year to direct this choir, and they don't charge us for the use of the kitchen or the fellowship hall for our dinners.

Outsider: That sure is generous of them! Who puts on these dinners that raise so much money?

Teen-ager: We do! Our dinners are always planned for a Friday night, because that's when a lot of people go out to eat and, besides, there's no school the next day so those of us who don't have Saturday jobs can sleep late. We come over on Thursday evening and do as much of the preparation as we can in advance. Three or four parents come and help us. On Friday night all twenty-one of us in the bell choir come to the church right after school. A couple of mothers usually come over about one o'clock to get the meat started and do a few other things. By five o'clock there are thirty to thirty-five of us here busy at work and we begin serving at five-fifteen. By seven or seven-thirty the last of our guests are leaving and we usually have everything cleaned up and we're ready to go home before nine o'clock.

Outsider: Now, tell me, who does all of this work?

Teen-ager: The kids and their parents. Every person in the choir is expected to be here *both* Thursday and Friday evenings and one parent must be here for *either* Thursday or Friday evening. We usually have about five or six parents come in to help on Thursday evening and the other fifteen to twenty come on Friday evening. Sometimes both parents come, but only one is required to work. We have four kids in the choir who come from single-parent homes and we've been careful not to do anything that would make them feel excluded.

Outsider: Did I hear you say at least one parent is *required* to work? Doesn't that exclude some of the youth because neither parent cares?

Director: Yes, that's one of our rules. No youngster may participate in the choir unless one parent is willing to work on these dinners.

Teen-ager: I don't know of any person who wanted to be in the bell choir who has been excluded because neither parent would work. We do have five kids in the choir who aren't from this parish. We have four kids in the choir who live with only one parent. We also have three or four who have parents that I rarely see in church on Sunday morning, but at least one parent has been here to work at every dinner. In fact, one couple who have a son in the choir, and who seldom come to church, both show up to work at our dinners and they're among our best workers!

Parent: In my opinion, this high level of parental involvement is what makes this work. Every youngster in the bell choir has the active support of at least one parent. Besides that, as the parents and kids work together, we develop a pretty close fellowship with one another.

Director: I trust you understand that while we have some very firm rules, and every young person is expected to live up to those rules, we don't run it like an army camp for recruits. We have lots of fun and we've a very close and caring fellowship. I'm forty-nine years old and I've survived raising two teen-agers. We have a seventeen-year-old still at home, so I think I know something about raising kids. That's our number one purpose. The bell choir is simply a way of doing that.

Parent: Please understand that we are not as rigid as we may sound. There are times when the family schedule will make it impossible for either parent to help with a dinner on either Thursday or Friday evening. We recognize that and we're flexible. Sometimes a couple will come and work Thursday and Friday nights to cover for some friends who can't make it. The next time their friends will work a double shift. We have high expectations for the parents, but we do make adjustments for various needs.

Teen-ager: One very important asset that we haven't mentioned so far is our director! Most of us are convinced that the key to making this whole thing work is that we all respect our director as an expert in directing a handbell choir, as a person, and as a friend. If we had an ordinary director, a lot of the kids probably would drift away and the whole thing might collapse.

Director: I appreciate the thought behind those words, but if I didn't have the cooperation of both the kids and their parents, I wouldn't do it.

Outsider: Is the handbell choir the only program here for senior high school youth?

Director: Oh, no! There is a Sunday morning church school class that usually has an attendance ranging between twelve and twenty. The regular senior high youth group meets at seven-thirty Sunday evening. Our handbell choir practices every Sunday evening from six-thirty to seven-thirty. We play on the third Sunday of every month, plus a dozen times a year for special events and programs. And, of course, we go on retreats, have parties and a lot of the kids go to summer church camp.

Outsider: How many senior high youth are in this parish?

Teen-ager: There are thirty-eight senior high youth who belong to this parish and sixteen are in the handbell choir. Five of the handbell choir members are not members of this congregation. Three of the five belong to other churches and two don't beong to any church. I believe all but three or four of the kids in our choir also stay for the Sunday evening youth fellowship or are in the Sunday school or both, but a lot of the kids participate in only one of these activities.

Outsider: I'm impressed!

Your assignment, as one who is interested in appraising youth ministries, is to list the general characteristics of this handbell choir that you believe might be useful in organizing a high school youth program in your church.

Here is the list one group came up with after they had listened to this conversation.

1. The youth are asked to make a clearly defined *and active* commitment to the program.

2. The youth are challenged by the high expectations of the program.

3. The ground rules are clearly defined.

4. The program provides for intergenerational cooperation.

5. There is a high level of *active* parental involvement in a form that nearly every parent can respond to by saying, "Yes, I can do that."

6. The youth gain a sense of satisfaction from learning and using a new skill. Sometimes this is referred to as "the discipline of the difficult."

7. The leader is a respected older adult.

8. The leader has had the benefit of being the parent of a teen-ager.

9. The leader has the respect of the parents.

10. The leader has the *active* support of the parents.

11. The salary gives the leader the satisfaction of being perceived as a part of the official staff of the parish and affirms the status of that role.

12. The leader is a competent and skilled person in this specialized field.

13. The leader likes youth.

14. The parents gain meaningful satisfactions from being an *active* support group for the program.

15. The parents become better acquainted with one another by working together.

16. The nature of the parental involvement opens the door for a set of family-to-family relationships to develop.

17. The expectations placed on the parents affirm the variety of family backgrounds.

18. The program involves the youth in a meaningful ministry.

19. The program gives high visibility to the youth.

20. The program encourages the active and visible support of the entire congregation *and* of the larger community.

21. This program is part of a larger design for youth ministries that affirms the idea of offering choices to youth.

22. The program is open to youth from non-member households.

23. The program is elitist. Those who participate feel they are part of a special group.

24. The program is financially self-supporting. The youth do not depend on the adult leadership to decide whether the scale of the program is consistent with the limitations of the parish budget.

25. The program is "owned" by the youth, not by an adult group.

26. The program offers a variety of affirmations and "strokes" for a good many people on many different occasions.

27. The program includes nine basic organizing principles that are very influential in turning a collection of fifteen to thirty persons into a closely knit and cohesive group. These are: (a) working together on a common and rewarding task, (b) music, (c) setting and attaining a specific, measurable, and attainable goal, (d) involvement in a shared and meaningful experience, (e) the continuity of a respected leader, (f) some degree of individual sacrifice on behalf of the group, (g) working as a team in which the success of the group is dependent on the contribution of every member, (h) being away together on overnight or longer trips, and (i) financial self-support.

28. The annual trip is a significant community-building experience for those who participate.

29. The annual trip provides the "reward" of fun, fellowship, and new experiences.

Now, can you add to that list?

How many of these factors can you build into the youth program in your congregation?

Are any of the items on your list in conflict with the values and the goals you have identified as foundation stones for youth ministries in your congregation? For example, how do you feel about the youth raising that much money every year? How do you respond to the high expectations placed on the parents? How do you feel about the elite character of this group? If any of the items on your list are in conflict, what adjustments will you have to make to reconcile these conflicts?

One of the value questions raised in this conversation at Trinity Church concerns the place of money-raising activities in a youth program. Before coming to a conclusion on this policy question, it may help to look at it from the perspective of some of today's youth.

Should We Permit Money-Raising Activities?

The exercise described on page 156 in which high school age youth are asked to identify all the components of the youth program in that congregation is one basis for appraising the place of money-raising activities in a youth program. We ask these teen-agers, "Now, let's look at this list we have on the board and decide which of the various activities and events are most dispensable. Let's cross out those items that you would be most willing to give up and reduce the list to the three or four essential components for a good basic youth program here in this church."

In four out of five churches in which we have completed this exercise, that final list, if both were on it in the beginning, includes (a) overnight or longer experiences such as choir trips, summer camp, retreats, or work-camp experiences, and (b) money-raising activities.

When asked why they gave such a high priority to raising money, the youth replied over and over again with responses such as these: "We think it's better if we raise the money necessary to finance our program ourselves rather than depend on the church to pay for it." "These money-raising activities provide the best opportunity for new kids in town to become a part of our group. Someone moves to town and on Saturday comes over and helps with the car wash. By the time that person leaves five or six hours later, we're all good friends and it's easy for that person to walk into our Sunday school class the next morning." "If we raise the money ourselves, we decide on the kind of trips we want to take. If we depended on the church to finance them, the budget committee would decide what kind of trips we should take." "If we didn't have the money-raising events, we would have to assess each kid a fee to cover the cost of a retreat or trip or activity and some of the kids couldn't afford it. This way no one is kept from participating because of the cost." "The money-raising activities here are more fun than anything else we do." "We can do more things than we could if we didn't have the money-raising programs."

If you are considering prohibiting money-raising activities for the youth program in your congregation, you may want to inquire and see if any of these values are shared by the teen-agers in your congregation. How can you reinforce those same values and still prohibit money-raising activities?

Can Youth Ministries Be Delegated?

"Two years ago we hired a college student to be our youth director on a part-time basis," explained Tom Ferrick, a long-time member of Calvary Church. "We thought that if we found someone young enough to relate to high school kids, we could rebuild the youth program. Our pastor is too busy to do it himself; and besides, he admits that youth work is not his special competence. We tried for a couple of years to get a young couple or two to take the responsibility, but that didn't seem to work. One young couple really was interesed in taking the leadership, but the wife's employer transferred her to Tennessee and we lost them. I think they might have been able to build a good youth program, but they moved after a few months. We made a few other attempts to recruit lay volunteers. When we didn't have any success, some of us got together and pushed through the idea of hiring a college student on a part-time basis to be our youth director. He's a fine young man, and very committed, but somehow he can't seem to get a response from the kids. Last week he said only six showed up for the Bible study group he started a month ago."

"You have to remember that the kids are awfully busy today," added Marie Brandt, the mother of a seventeen-year-old son. "The school expects a lot of homework, and at least half of them have part-time jobs that take fifteen to twenty hours a week."

"I still think the key is the pastor," argued Henry Schmidt. "If the pastor is able and willing to accept the responsibilities for working with youth, you'll have a good program. If he isn't, you won't. It's as simple as that!"

That conversation, which may sound familiar to many readers, is based on an assumption that deserves to be reexamined. Can a parish delegate youth ministries to one or two persons? Is it reasonable to expect a part-time youth director or a couple of lay volunteers or the pastor or an associate minister to take the central responsibility for youth ministries?

A great many congregations operate under the assumption that the responsibility of youth ministries can be delegated to one or two or three adults. Over the years, however, we have accumulated some evidence that has caused us to challenge that assumption. The beginning point in this discussion is in the question, Who is the primary client for the youth program?

The source of this challenge (to the assumption that youth ministries can be delegated to a few persons) is the belief that the youth are the primary clients for any specialized ministry with teen-agers and that therefore, their opinion should carry some weight.

During the past several years, we have had the opportunity to ask more than twenty-two-hundred high school students a question that can be addressed to the youth in your congregation. This exercise takes about twenty minutes and is not difficult. After we gather a group of teen-agers, we introduce the subject in these words:

"Here is a list of adult roles that may be filled by persons who have some official responsibility for the youth program in this congregation. We are not going to take the time now to debate the relative importance of each of these roles or responsibilities. What we would like you to do is to take one of these sheets of paper and, individually without consulting anyone else, write opposite each role the name of one adult who has official responsibilities here for the youth program and who fills that role for you.

"This might be a Sunday school teacher, a lay volunteer who is a counselor or adviser with the youth program, a member of the youth council, the pastor, a paid staff person, or any adult you believe fills that role. You may write the same name opposite each role, or you may pick a different person for each role or you may leave some blank. You may list one person opposite each of two or three or more of these roles or any combination you want that will help us understand whom you see filling these various responsibilities here in this congregation. All we ask is that you limit yourself to the names of persons who have official responsibilities for the youth program here."

The sheet of paper contains this list of roles: teacher, friend, counselor, big brother or big sister, recreation leader, executive secretary or organizer, pastor, advocate, model of an adult Christian.

We take a few minutes to define each term. For example, the advocate is the adult who supports and interprets the teen-ager's point of view when a controversial issue or program surfaces. Everyone knows what a friend is. The executive secretary is the adult who looks after the details, helps organize and implement the youth program, and makes sure the necessary arrangements for a special event or trip are not overlooked. The big brother or big sister is an adult who fills the role of an older sibling. The counselor is an adult whom a teen-ager might seek out for advice and counsel. The last role on the list refers to the adult that you might model your life after as you think about your commitment as a Christian.

We have completed this exercise with groups ranging in size from five to thirty teen-agers in more than two hundred churches of all sizes from eleven different denominations. The results have been amazingly consistent with two important exceptions. There were five consistent patterns.

First, and perhaps most significant, despite the repeated admonitions to list only adults *who have official responsibilities for the youth program*, most of the teen-agers will include at least one or two names of persons who subsequently categorically deny they have anything to do with the youth program in that church. Frequently, an adult who is not related to the youth program is identified as friend or model of an adult Christian or advocate. In several churches the semi-retired part-time minister of visitation, who when interviewed disclaimed any relationship to the youth program, was identified by several of the teen-agers as their friend or as pastor or as a model of an adult Christian or as the counselor.

Second, in those congregations where all the adult leaders agreed that the responsibility for the youth program has been delegated to one person (such as the youth director or a lay volunteer or the associate minister), the youth responded with a different version of reality. The usual pattern was that one adult was listed opposite two or three or, occasionally, four roles on each sheet of paper and each teen-ager identified other adults for the remaining role or left them blank.

When this happened, the usual pattern was that the youth director or youth minister was identified with the same two or three or four roles on paper after paper. It was rare for that one person to be identified more than once with the other three or four or five roles on the sheet.

Third, in those congregations in which the adult leaders assumed that a full-time staff person (such as the pastor or the director of Christian education or the associate director) was in charge of the youth program, the respondents usually identified the young (under age thirty) staff person with such roles as friend or big brother or big sister or executive secretary or recreation leader.

When the staff person identified by the adult leaders as the person in charge of our youth program was past forty years of age, the teen-agers tended to identify that person with such roles as teacher or counselor or pastor or model of an adult Christian or advocate. Perhaps some of these roles are suited for younger adult leaders, and others for older staff leadership?

A fourth pattern was revealed in what appeared to be the congregations with the best youth programs. In these congregations the names of many different adults appeared on these sheets. By contrast, in those parishes in which the youth program appeared to be inadequate or weak, it was not uncommon for the sheets of paper to be returned with only one or two names on the paper and two or three or four roles left blank.

Finally, in the larger congregations, in which the professional staff included two or three or more program persons (pastor, director of Christian education, youth director, associate minister, minister of visitation) plus two or three secretaries, it was not uncommon for most of these staff members to be listed at least once or twice on many of the sheets of paper turned in by the youth.

These are congregations that tend to emphasize the delegation of responsibilities to specialists, yet many of the youth felt each staff member played an important role in the youth program. It was a big surprise to many senior pastors when they discovered how frequently their names appeared on these sheets alongside other ministers on the staff.

There were two exceptions to these generalizations that may be worth noting. First, in the smaller congregations (fewer than seventy-five at worship on Sunday morning), it was not uncommon for most of the teen-agers to list only the names of the same two or three lay volunteers and the pastor. Perhaps they were more obedient to the instructions to limit the list to the names of adults with official responsibilities for the youth program. Or perhaps this occurred because smaller congregations tend to be more relational and larger churches tend to be functional?

The other major exception was found in the very large congregations with a full-time staff member who carried the portfolio for youth ministries. In several of these congregations a fivefold pattern surfaced: (a) the teen-agers who were most active in the youth program were very enthusiastic about the ministry of that staff person; (b) that person's name was written in opposite five to eight roles on the sheets turned in by these actively involved youngsters, but very few other adults were listed; (c) the role most often left blank was model of an adult Christian, (d) two-thirds to nine-tenths of the high school youth in these large parishes were not actively involved in the youth program, and (e) the parents of these youth who were not involved tended to blame themselves and/or their children for the fact that their teen-agers did not participate.

Is it reasonable, then, to expect one staff member to be able to relate effectively to thirty-five or fifty or more youth?

In reflecting on these responses, and on subsequent conversations with the youth who shared in these experiences, three concluding observations need to be lifted up.

First, the entire exercise is based on the assumption that adult role models are very important. One of the most influential dimensions of any ministry with children or youth is providing attractive role models. An argument can be made that the most significant decision any congregation makes in developing a ministry with youth is in the selection of adult role models.

Second, it is assumed that all nine of the adult roles identified in this exercise are important and meaningful roles in any ministry with youth. The most important probably is the one labeled model of an adult Christian.

Finally, these responses suggest very strongly that from a youth perspective, it is unrealistic to expect any one adult (or even two or three) to be able to fill all of these roles with even a majority of the teen-agers. That suggests, from a congregational perspective, that it might be more realistic to think about developing a team of adults to work with youth, rather than attempting to delegate that responsibility to one person.

What is the policy in your congregation on delegating youth ministries to a very small number of people? How is it working?

Who Offers the Mountaintop Experiences?

"I'll never forget that campfire on the last evening of summer camp when I was seventeen years old," recalled the fifty-seven-year-old pastor. "It was forty years ago last month that I made the commitment to give my life to Christ and to enter the Christian ministry. I've never faced a really difficult decision since that evening and I have no regrets."

"The most important single thing the church ever did for me was what happened at summer camp when I was a teen-ager," reflected the chemistry professor at a state university. "The last night at camp was always planned to be a mountaintop experience for us. Those commitment services have had a greater impact on my life than anything I've ever experienced including Vietnam, graduate school, and becoming a parent. Do they still offer kids those kinds of experiences today?"

One of the most significant questions to be raised as you appraise the youth program in your church should be about these mountaintop experiences. Who offers them?

Perhaps one congregation in twenty is large enough and has sufficient resources to do this unilaterally in a weekend retreat or a summer camp. For the other nineteen out of twenty, the answer usually will be either "That's one of the things we do cooperatively with other churches" or "We don't do that."

For many congregations the planning and scheduling of the large scale youth rally that includes a call to commitment may be the most important single contribution the regional judicatory or the national youth office can offer. Does your denomination offer these events for youth? If not, what can you do to change that? Or have you concluded that mountaintop experiences no longer are important or relevant?

13

THE WEEKDAY NURSERY SCHOOL

"The next item on the agenda is a request from the board of the nursery school for an extension of their contract," declared the presiding officer at the monthly meeting of the governing board of the Orchard Ridge Church. "Their current three-year contract for use of our building expires next June, and they are asking for a three-year extension on the same terms."

"I move that we direct the trustees to go ahead and extend the contract for another three years," offered the fifty-nine-year-old Eunice Swanson, a charter member of this twenty-eight-year-old congregation and one of the persons who had helped organize the nursery school a decade earlier.

"I'll second the motion to get this subject before us," added Harry Brown, "but I know a lot of our members are not in favor of keeping it here."

"How many new families have we received as members because of the nursery school?" asked Evelyn VanderMeer. "My understanding years ago was that we expected this to be a vital part of our evangelistic thrust into the community."

"I can't tell you exactly," replied Eunice Swanson. "People join a church for a variety of reasons, not just one factor. I would guess at least three or four families who are now members had their first contact with this church through the nursery school. It might even be as many as seven or eight. I don't believe anyone can answer that question exactly."

"I don't think that is a relevant question," interrupted Terry Evans who served as the liaison to the nursery school board. "The nursery school was never intended to attract a lot of new members. It's primarily a service to the community. The nursery school is a part of our Christian witness in this community, not a part of our new member recruitment system."

"Is religion taught in the nursery school?" inquired Ruth Bosetti. "Do the children learn any Bible verses? Someone told me that during the week the teachers remove all the pictures of Jesus from the walls in the rooms they use."

"Before I can make an intelligent decision on this motion, I need to know how much this is costing us," demanded Bruce Harrison. "How large is our subsidy to the school?"

"Is there anyone who doesn't want the contract renewed?" innocently asked George Mitchell. "Does anyone want us to terminate this relationship?"

"I can name three Sunday school teachers who would be delighted if we did not renew the contract," quickly responded another member of the governing body in a highly emotional tone of voice. "I expect they may not volunteer for another year as teachers unless they regain at least some control over the rooms to which they are assigned on Sunday."

"Pastor, what's your opinion on this?" inquired the church treasurer. "I understand that you and the director have had some rather severe differences of opinion."

"Has anyone asked the trustees how they feel about this?" asked another person. "If I understand the motion before us correctly, it directs the trustees to renew the contract. Perhaps we should ask them if they want to extend the contract."

These questions and comments represent many of the emotions and concerns that are evoked by the presence of a weekday nursery school. They should not be dismissed lightly. They represent some strongly held opinions! It may be more useful, however, in appraising the weekday nursery school housed in your building to reflect on a series of questions directed at the central purpose and the philosophy of that program.

1. Is it a service program or a ministry?

The most important single question to ask in appraising a weekday nursery school is directed at the reason it originally was organized. Most of those housed in church buildings fall into one of three categories.

A substantial number were organized by a director and/or a group of parents. They looked for a place to house this program for young children. Sooner or later they found a congregation that owned the necessary facilities and was open to the idea of making these rooms available to the nursery school. The usual outcome was a landlord-tenant relationship. In many churches the congregation became a benevolent landlord and a supporter of the weekday program. In others an adversary relationship emerged as the years passed.

In another group of churches the initiative for creating the nursery school came from within the congregation. Usually it was conceptualized as a service program to serve residents of the community by filling an unmet need. Typically, a special committee was created to recruit a director, organize the program, acquire the basic equipment and supplies, contact the potential clientele and secure the initial financing. In these congregations the nursery school often is understood by most members to be one of several programs offered by that church. Among the big differences, however, are these. First, while it is assumed that at least nine out of ten persons attending Sunday morning worship will come from member households, no one is surprised when a majority of the children in the weekday program come from non-member families. Second, while it is widely assumed that many of the non-members who are regular attenders at Sunday morning worship are prospective future members, it is not assumed that the non-member parents sending their children to the nursery school are prospective future members. Third, while it is assumed that most of the costs of the Sunday school will be borne by the congregation as a whole, it is widely accepted that the parents of the children enrolled will carry most of the costs of the weekday nursery school. Fourth, while it is understood that all of the teachers in the Sunday church school will be committed Christians who are members of that congregation, these are not influential criteria in the selection of teachers for the weekday nursery school. Fifth, while it is often assumed the pastor will be heavily involved in the educational ministry of that congregation, rarely does anyone expect the pastor to be involved in the weekday nursery school.

Most of the weekday nursery schools that fit into either of these first two categories fit into the role of a service program to the community. They parallel the food bank to feed the hungry, the cooperative arrangement with other churches to respond to the emergency needs of transients, the decision to allow a local chapter of Alcoholics Anonymous to meet in the building one evening a week or the use of the fellowship hall by an aerobic dance class. They are largely· self-sufficient programs that are not conceptualized as a part of the core ministries of that congregation.

The third and smallest category includes those churches in which the weekday nursery school was created as an expansion of either the educational program of that congregation and/or as an integral part of a total ministry to young families. The distinctions among these three origins of the nursery school will be illustrated by subsequent questions in this self-appraisal exercise.

What were the origins of the nursery school housed in your building? Today is it primarily a service program to the general community? Or is it an integral part of the educational and/or evangelistic ministry of your congregation?

2. Who is the client?

Most nursery schools housed in church buildings appear to have been designed on the premise that the child is the number one client. In these weekday schools there is very little contact between most of the parents and the staff of the school. The parents register their children, pay the tuition fees, and provide transportation and that about completes the parental responsibilities.

In a few cases it is clear the director was seeking to launch a new enterprise and the director is the number one client. The design of the program, the leadership role of the director, the fee schedule, the educational philosophy, the organizational structure, the compensation for teachers, the weekly and daily schedule, the treaty with the congregation housing the enterprise, and the ownership of the equipment and materials support the assumption the director is the number one client.

In a fair number of nongeographical parishes the skeptic can be persuaded that the original client may have been the conscience of the congregation. A reconstruction of history suggests that the initial motivation for launching the weekday nursery school was the conviction that "we must do something to serve all the young children in this neighborhood." Or it may have been summarized in the reflection, "After we finished our new building some of us felt guilty over all these nice new rooms setting here vacant all week, so we found this woman who was looking for a place for her school. The arrangement we worked out with her satisfied her needs and also relieved our guilt."

In approximately 1 or 2 percent of the weekday nursery schools housed in church buildings the primary client is the entire family including that preschool child. This is reflected by the fact that the weekday program is one part of a constellation of ministries, programs, events, classes, and activities directed at the entire family. Examples range from classes on parenting to a Sunday morning Bible study group for young parents to a children's sermon during the Sunday morning worship service to a choir for young children to a circle in the women's organization for mothers of young children to the expectation that young children will be in attendance at Sunday morning worship to the Wednesday afterschool youth club that includes "graduates" of the weekday program to marriage enrichment retreats to an expectation that parents will serve as volunteer helpers in the weekday school to Sunday school classes for older siblings to eight or ten family nights a year to a "birthday party for Jesus" at three P.M. on December 24 for children too young to come to the Christmas Eve service to a parent-teacher organization for the nursery school.

Who is the number one client for the weekday nursery school in your church?

3. Is Christianity taught?

Perhaps the most controversial question to ask is whether religion will be taught to the young children in the nursery school. Will they memorize Bible verses? Will they listen to Bible stories? Most important of all, will the staff by their actions and attitudes, as well as by their words, witness to their faith as Christians? Nearly all Protestant churches expect every program staff member not only to be a committed Christian but also to be an articulate evangelist of the Christian faith. Will a similar standard be applied to persons who teach in the Sunday school? In the weekday nursery school?

A remarkably large number of nursery school directors and teachers are convinced it is wrong to teach religion to three-year-old and four-year-old children.[1] While they do not hesitate to impose on young and impressionable children their own convictions on such subjective matters as interpersonal relationships, punctuality, nutrition, attitudes toward adults, dress, patriotism, art, pronunciation of words in the English language, music, grammar, boy-girl relationships, cooperation, posture, behavior, and health care, they protest it is wrong to teach religion to young children. Is religion taught in the nursery school housed in your church? If so, what religion? If not, who made that decision?

4. What is the weekly schedule?

A typical nursery school housed in a church building may advertise a schedule of Tuesday and Thursday for three-year-olds and Monday, Wednesday, and Friday for four-year-olds. The obvious implication behind this schedule is that the weekday program is unrelated to the Sunday morning church school. If parents want to have their children attend that parish's Sunday school, the burden is on the parent to take the initiative to arrange it.

Perhaps 1 percent of the nursery schools housed in church buildings advertise Sunday-Tuesday-Thursday for three-year-olds and Sunday-Monday-Wednesday-Friday for four-year-olds. The obvious message is that the weekday program is an integral part of the total educational ministry with young children. Many of these churches add a note that if the parents do not want their child to participate in a Christian Sunday school class, they are free to enroll the youngster for only the weekday sessions, but add that the child will miss part of the total program by being absent on Sunday. These churches also often attempt to build in a high degree of continuity between the Sunday school and the weekday program by having the same teachers meet the same children in the same room at approximately the same hour. Normally the tuition charge is the same whether the child attends on Sunday or is absent. These churches see the weekday program as a part of the total Christian ministry and do not pretend that it is a secular service program.

What is the schedule for your nursery school? What are the assumptions underlying that schedule?

5. What is the line of accountability?

The typical weekday nursery school housed in a church building has a board that oversees the school. Usually the majority of the members are parents of children, including many parents who are not members of that congregation. In several parts of the country the board includes adults who are not self-identified Christians. Sometimes the host church has members who are not parents on the board.

Several of the entrepreneurial nursery schools do not have a governing board. The director has complete control of the school and is not accountable to any agency or board as long as minimum state requirements are met.

In most of the congregations in which the weekday nursery is conceptualized as an integral part of the ministry and outreach of that church, the lines of accountability tend to be clearer. One arrangement is for the weekday program to be under the oversight of the Christian education committee. Another is for it to be under the direct supervision of the council or session or central governing body for that congregation. A third is for the line of accountability to run from the nursery school to the pastor or to some other full-time staff person responsible for program.

In those congregations in which nearly every program area has a distinctive evangelistic thrust, the nursery school may be accountable to the evangelism committee. What are the lines of accountability in your church?

6. Who hires the director and the teachers?

Another dimension of this issue of accountability concerns the selection and tenure of the staff of the nursery school. Who selects the director? Who recruits and hires the teachers? Who formulates the criteria for eligibility? What are the lines of accountability for the staff? To the director? To the board of the nursery school? To the pastor? To a personnel committee? To the Christian education committee?

Who selected the staff for your nursery school? What were the criteria? (Note: This issue can raise highly divisive questions over control and accountability!)

7. What is the relationship of the director to the pastor?

This question overlaps the previous two issues on accountability. A common answer is that the director and the pastor see themselves as adversaries. This is especially common when the nursery school is completely separate from the total ministry of that congregation and the institutional relationship is one of landlord and tenant.

In a few congregations the pastor is in a position analogous to the superintendent of the public school system while the director of the nursery school is the equivalent of the principal of a small elementary school.

In several large congregations the director of the weekday nursery school holds other program responsibilities (such as children's ministries) and/or is perceived as simply one of several staff persons responsible for specialized ministries, all of whom are accountable to the program coordinator or the senior minister.

8. What is the financial relationship?

Four responses to that question cover most of the nursery schools housed in church buildings today.

Perhaps the most common is for the nursery school to have its own treasurer, its own budget, and its own bank account. The nursery school is expected to have sufficient income to cover all the operating costs of the weekday program such as salaries, supplies, equipment, liability insurance, telephone, janitorial services, and its share of the costs for heat and light. The host congregation covers all capital costs plus property insurance and maintenance. In these churches the receipts and expenditures of the nursery school do not appear in the financial reports of the congregation.

The second most common arrangement is for the host congregation to supply the physical facilities including the outdoor playground and also cover part of the operating costs. Sometimes this is done through direct grants, sometimes through scholarships to enable the children of lower income families to participate.

Less common are those churches in which the nursery school is an integral part of the educational ministry of that congregation and the receipts and expenditures of the nursery school are carried in the budget of the Christian education committee. In these congregations it is rare to hear anyone ask such questions as, "Are we making or losing money on our Sunday school?" "Is that Tuesday evening Bible study group that meets in the parlor paying its way?" "Do the receipts from the weekday nursery school cover all the expenditures it incurs?" "Which of the adult classes are being subsidized?"

A fourth, and relatively rare pattern is for the congregation to be financially dependent on the weekday nursery. The nursery school pays out of its receipts a disproportionately large share of the operating expenses of that congregation. If the nursery school suddenly closed, that congregation would have difficulty meeting its monthly bills for utilities, insurance, janitorial services, and supplies!

What is the financial relationship of the weekday nursery school to your congregation? Who subsidizes whom? Does everyone concerned agree on that? Are the facts consistent with the policies?

9. Is it a nursery school or an early childhood development center?

Perhaps the biggest single change in this area of ministry has been the evolution of the whole concept in less than two decades. In hundreds of congregations the weekday nursery school founded in the 1960s has evolved into a sophisticated center concerned with the physical, social, moral, intellectual, cultural, religious, and personal development of the young child.

This change has been stimulated by the tremendous increase in the number of persons with specialized educational training in early childhood development.

The churches that house an early childhood development center usually offer a far broader range of opportunities for members of the family that includes a preschool child than does the typical nursery school that follows the model established back in the 1960s.

What does your church house? Does the director have specialized training in early childhood development? Are prospective teachers expected to have a degree in early childhood development? Or are they expected to take courses in this specialized field as part of their continuing education?

10. Who are the allies and auxiliaries?

The weekday nursery schools that are organized as service programs to the general community usually fall into one of three categories in response to this question. In some the director runs it. In many more the nursery school board is the chief ally for the school. In others a board oversees the school and a parental group helps support and nurture the program.

The array of allies often is far greater in those churches in which the weekday nursery school is viewed as a part of the total ministry of that congregation. Examples include: (a) the Christian education committee, (b) the pastor or program director who carries staff responsibilities for the nursery school, (c) the choir director or minister of music who teaches music in the weekday school, (d) the Grandfathers' Club that fixes equipment, buys toys, installs the fence around the outdoor playground, and in general runs interference for the weekday program, a group that often includes mature men who do not have their own grandchildren in the school but serve as surrogate grandfathers, (e) the parent-teacher's organization, (f) the women's organization in the church that supplies money for scholarships for children who otherwise could not attend and/or purchases equipment for the nursery school, (g) the Sunday school leaders who see the weekday program as an enriching ally, not as a competitor for space and supplies, (h) the Grandmother's Club that furnishes volunteers to help with the nursery school, (i) the "graduates" from a few years earlier who now offer role models to the children in the nursery school on what this congregation offers them when they are a few years older, (j) the members of the evangelism committee who view the weekday nursery school as an essential component of their outreach to parents of young children, or (k) an adult Sunday school class that adopts the nursery school as its special outreach project.

Who are the allies of that nursery school housed in your building?

11. What are the financial barriers?

Very few churches place a financial barrier before an adult who would like to come and participate in the corporate worship of God. An offering may be received, but no one is required to contribute. Very few churches require the children attending Sunday school to financially support that ministry.

Most nursery schools housed in church buildings, however, do place a substantial financial expectation before any parent who wants to enroll a child in that weekday program. This is almost universal in the entrepreneurial nursery schools.

In those congregations in which the nursery school is conceptualized as a part of the total ministry of that congregation, systematic efforts frequently are made to lower that barrier. The typical response is to provide scholarships for those children who otherwise could not afford to participate. Sometimes funds are provided to the congregational budget for this purpose. In other churches bequests provide the necessary funds. In some congregations an adult group, such as an adult Sunday school class or the men's fellowship or the women's organization adopt this as part of their purpose and reason for being. In a few churches a special second-mile appeal is made once a year for money to finance these scholarships.

What are the financial barriers to enrollment to the weekday nursery school housed in your building? What can be done to reduce that barrier? Who will take the initiative?

12. Who determines policy?

Now comes what may be the most difficult question on this list. If your self-appraisal committee concludes that significant changes should be made in the purpose, role, operation, financing, or conceptual framework of the weekday nursery school housed in your building, who has the authority to suggest those changes? The governing board of the congregation? The Christian education committee? The pastor?

One church, for example, wanted to adopt the nursery school, which for eight years had been a semi-autonomous service program housed in that congregation's building, and convert it into one component of a package of ministries with young families. The director of the nursery school, however, made it very clear that she did not want to be adopted. She did not want religion taught in the weekday program. She did not want the nursery school to be accountable to anyone except the board she had created and selected. She did not want the names of the parents to be entered on the evangelism committee's list of prospective new members. She did not want the nursery school budget to become a part of the budget of the Christian education committee. She did not want anyone to have a voice in the selection of the teachers. She was and is an influential member of that congregation. Her husband is a third-generation member from an influential family in that congregation.

When faced with a choice that appeared to be gaining control of the weekday nursery school and losing a prominent family or leaving the status quo untouched, the governing board of that congregation chose to leave the status quo alone.

Who would make that decision in your congregation? What decision would they make? Why?

14

Questions for the Building Planning Committee

One of the most frequently played indoor sports in the churches is to blame yesterday's building committee for the mistakes, oversights, and omissions in designing the structure that houses today's congregation. If your congregation is involved in a construction or remodeling program, it may be useful to develop a checklist of questions to be asked about the design of the proposed building project. Some of these questions will emerge from the sense of need that generated the current proposal. Others can be generated by visiting churches that have completed similar construction programs and by talking with the leaders as they reflect on their experience. A third source is to see which of the questions in this chapter should be asked about your plans. These questions have been derived from visits to several hundred congregations that were involved in building programs during the past quarter century. This is not intended to be a manual on building design, only to lift up questions that frequently have been overlooked.

The Evangelistic Outreach

The best beginning point is to ask several questions about how the proposed construction program will affect the evangelistic outreach of this congregation.

1. Will the stranger tend to identify the building as the meeting place of a religious congregation or as a school or as an office building or as a medical center? Does it look like a church? If it does not, what are the design considerations that will help a stranger identify it as the meeting house for a Christian congregation?

2. Where will the exterior cross be displayed? How visible will it be to the motorist in a passing automobile?

3. Does the location, site, and design lend itself to the possibility

that one wall of the building can carry the name of the congregation so it will be readily identifiable to passing motorists?

4. Is the entrance into the driveway from the street into the parking area highly visible, safe, and easy to negotiate?

5. Do you have space to have a separate entrance and a separate exit (preferably from different streets) in order to facilitate traffic flow on the peak-hour-of-use occasions?

6. Are at least three or four parking spaces that are near the main entrance reserved for and designated for visitors?

7. Where will the sign or bulletin board *outside* the building be located? Can it be read by the driver of a passing car who is on the other side of the street?

8. Is the main entrance for those coming to Sunday morning worship obviously the main entrance? Or do you fool people with an attractive set of double doors on one side of the building, but nearly all of the oldtimers come in from the parking lot through an obscure door on the other side? Does that inhibit members from greeting visitors?

Hundreds of church buildings, including many constructed since 1965, have an impressive set of double doors leading from the street into the narthex, but nearly all of the regulars enter on Sunday morning through an obscure entrance from the parking lot in the rear. Does the *real* entrance proclaim, "Folks, this is the correct way to enter this building on Sunday morning"?

9. Will *exterior* directional signs be needed to help the stranger find the appropriate door? Examples include signs for worship, church school, office, nursery, and fellowship hall.

10. After a stranger has entered the building, will interior directional signs be needed to help that person find the appropriate room? Examples include the thin red line on the wall that leads to the three-year-old room or the thin green line that leads to the nursery or the blue line that leads to the office or lettered signs that direct people to worship, the educational wing, the fellowship hall, and other places.

11. Is there a spacious area immediately outside that main entrance in which strangers can be greeted as they enter before they go to the sanctuary?

12. Does the design of the building encourage people to go directly outside following worship or go to an interior fellowship or

socializing area where people are encouraged by the physical setting to greet one another, to welcome strangers, and to linger for a while before leaving?

13. If the building includes an office for the minister, is this clearly identifiable from the point at which a stranger would begin to look for the minister on a Tuesday morning?

14. For congregations interested in reaching the mothers of young children the most important room often is the nursery. Does the design provide for an attractive, ground-level, well-lighted, and spacious nursery that will be an inviting place for mothers of young children? (The 1980s brought a new record in the number of women giving birth to their first child.)

15. Do the plans include a nursery for babies and a separate room for toddlers? Do these include the necessary counters, storage areas, sinks, and toilets? Are they located (a) near the main entrance, (b) above ground (not in the basement which encourages mold), (c) not near the furnace or heating plant, and (d) easily accessible from a room used for adult meetings.

16. Do the plans include an attractive, inviting, and easy-to-keep-clean women's restroom? (This is very important for those congregations seeking to reach the generation born after 1945 who grew up in a world that includes attractive restrooms for women.)

17. Do the plans include a room in which brides can prepare for the wedding? (Note: The number of marriages during each year of the 1980s will be nearly double the annual figures for the 1955-60 era.)

18. Does the design inhibit the flow of communication and conceal program? Many of the buildings designed two or three decades ago "hide" many important programs at the far end or on the second floor or in the basement. As a result many members and most visitors leave with a very limited understanding of the scope of the total program.

19. Does the design reinforce values and goals? Some educators are convinced that modeling is the most influential pedagogical approach used in the churches today. This suggests that an important factor in strengthening the children's division of the Sunday school is for children to see adults, and especially adult males, involved in adult Sunday school classes. Does the proposed

design encourage children to see adults engaged in study on Sunday morning?

20. Does the design include meeting the needs of persons with handicapping conditions?[1]

Interrelationships

A second set of questions should be raised about the use of the building by ordinary human beings in the last quarter of the twentieth century.

1. What is the pedestrian traffic pattern for persons coming to and leaving worship? Does the design include several attractive exits, making it impossible for the pastor to greet more than a small fraction of the worshipers? Or does the design funnel people from the nave through one doorway into a large corridor or a hall that encourages milling around and socializing before people leave the building? (Obviously many very large congregations will be more concerned with the flow of traffic than with enabling everyone to be greeted by the pastors and therefore may need two or three exits from the nave, but these are fewer than 10 percent of all congregations.)

The extra exits necessary to meet safety standards should be made as unattractive as possible to discourage people from bypassing the minister or from ignoring one another. (One way to accomplish this is to have these secondary exits from the sanctuary be as distant as possible from the parking lot. Another is to have them open out onto a discouraging walk area that will require them to hurdle shrubbery in order to reach the parking lot or a sidewalk.)

2. Will the design of the chancel enable the minister to enter or exit from the chancel unobtrusively?

3. Does the design enable choir members to enter or exit the choir area inconspicuously?

4. Is the plan for corporate worship designed to convey the impression of a "good crowd today" regardless of the number in attendance?

The simplest way to accomplish this is with chairs or movable pews so the number of seats can be changed from week to week or event to event. It is possible to design a setting for corporate worship that conveys the impression of a full house whether the number in attendance is one hundred, two hundred, or three hundred. The key variable is *not* the size of the room, but rather the number and placement of the chairs or pews. The basic generalization is to provide seats for 95 percent of the anticipated number who will be in attendance. The desired result is, "We had such a big crowd we had to bring in extra chairs."

5. Does the design include *at least* one general purpose meeting room with carpet on the floor for each two hundred members? Could this room also serve as the meeting space for the council or board or session or consistory or vestry? An attractive meeting room is a simple means of increasing the regularity of attendance by the members of that group.

6. If there are two or more of these rooms, are they different in size in order to accommodate different size groups?

7. Will some of these rooms actually turn out to be informal corridors as people take a shortcut through that room to go from one part of the building to another? Can that be avoided?

8. Do the plans include a room that can be used as a television studio for taping programs for cable TV?

9. Is there a room or a semi-private area that will enable people to make private telephone calls from this building?

10. Does the design meet state and local building code requirements if this congregation should decide to house a weekday early childhood development center? In many states the requirements for all-day programming for children are stricter than for Sunday school use. These requirements may include a fenced outdoor play area, a direct exit to the outdoors from each room, restrooms, a wet sink in each room, and a sprinkler system.

11. Is the kitchen sufficiently large that several people can work there at the same time *and enjoy one another's company* or is it so small that the presence of several people at the same time will endgender hostility?

12. Does the design include a room for the choir to gather in and rehearse on Sunday morning without interfering with Sunday school classes?

Weekday Use

A third set of questions reflects the concerns of those who will work in and visit the building during the week.

1. Are there at least a half dozen parking spaces close to an entrance for the convenience of those who must arrive when it is raining?

2. Is there a meeting room or parlor on the ground floor for the convenience of those who must attend a meeting during the week, but who find it difficult to climb stairs?

3. Is the area for persons waiting to see the pastor separate from the church secretary's work area? Sometimes people feel obligated to engage the church secretary in conversation while waiting to see the minister.

4. Is there a direct exit from the pastor's office to the parking area for persons who want privacy following a counseling session with the minister?

5. If the staff includes a pastoral counselor, does that office have a direct outside exit?

6. Are the work areas for volunteers separate from the work areas for staff so unnecessary interference with another's work can be minimized?

7. Will the church secretary or receptionist be able to see the main entrance for weekday use to enable someone to visually monitor persons entering or leaving the building?

8. Is there a clear and unmistakable entrance to the office area that weekday visitors cannot miss?

9. Is there an exterior sign that directs weekday visitors to the office area?

10. Will the design of the structure enable only one entrance door to be unlocked for weekday use?

11. Does the office area include (a) all offices, (b) one meeting room, and (c) restrooms so only that one section of the building will need to be heated or cooled to the comfort level for weekday use? Is that cluster of rooms located near what will be the main weekday entrance and exit?

12. Will the receptionist or church secretary have a separate work area with a counter or dutch door separating the receptionist from strangers?

In other words, is there at least a modest physical barrier that separates the church secretary from (a) persons waiting to see the pastor, (b) members who drop by "to see how things are going," (c) volunteers who are carrying out their volunteer assignments,

(d) the bookkeeper or financial secretary, (e) strangers who stop in for a handout, and (f) staff members who are passing through that area. In general, it is *not* a good idea to combine into one large room the secretary's office, the waiting room for people wanting to see the minister, a fellowship corner for visitors and staff, the receptionist's work area, and the entrance to the offices of the program staff.

13. Do the plans include a separate workroom for duplicating equipment, office machines, storage? Does this room have a door that closes it off completely? Does it have an extension telephone? Does it have a wet sink?

14. If the need, either current or future, calls for two or more church secretaries, bookkeepers, computer operators, word processors, will the design enable each one to have a separate work area with a reasonable degree of privacy? This is of critical importance for the bookkeeper or computer operator!

15. If the staff includes both a church secretary (or pastor's secretary) and a receptionist, will the design of the office area enable the receptionist to greet visitors and answer the telephone without intruding on the private work area of the church secretary?

16. Does the design include space for the future addition of another program staff member, either part-time or full-time, and a private office for that person?

17. Are the walls and doors of the pastor's office soundproof so all conversation will be private? This usually requires a double-door entrance into the pastor's study.

18. Is the pastor's office sufficiently large to accommodate meetings of five to seven persons or more?

19. For those churches seeking to reach parents of young children, is the nursey convenient to that first floor general purpose meeting room?

20. Is there a drinking fountain on each floor?

21. Does the design call for a wet sink on each floor? The custodian will explain why this is important.

22. While this will strike many leaders as a functional issue, rather than a matter of staff relationships, the location of the restrooms should be given careful concern. If everyone on the staff has to leave the office area and go out into a common corridor to reach a restroom, this encourages chance encounters in the

corridor and brief conversations, and in general enhances staff relationships. If the design includes one or two private restrooms and/or discourages corridor traffic, this may enhance privacy, save time, improve efficiency, increase alienation, eliminate those casual conversations, and require more scheduled staff meetings.

23. It also should be noted that intrastaff communication tends to be inhibited if (a) offices are more than seventy-five feet apart and/or (b) offices are located on different floors and/or (c) corridor traffic does not go past a particular staff office, such as the office at the end of the corridor.

24. Does the design include sloping floors? (Many mature adults find it difficult to walk on sloping floors.)

25. Are the walls between meeting rooms or classrooms soundproofed so one group will not interfere with another meeting at the same hour?

26. For the benefit of those who have difficulty climbing stairs, does the ground floor include (a) at least one general purpose meeting room, (b) restrooms, (c) a room for corporate worship, (d) the pastor's office.

27. If a future decision is made to secure a person who will both play the organ and direct the choir, does the design make this difficult or easy?

28. In the very large congregations averaging more than three hundred or four hundred at worship, large group events can be a very important factor in strengthening the sense of community and reinforcing cohesion. Will the fellowship hall accommodate at tables at least one-half as many people as can be accommodated at one worship service? If not, what are the alternatives for large group events?

The Trustees' Concerns

The trustees or the property committee may or may not have an influential voice in the design of the building, but they will have the responsibility for the care of the structure after it is completed. Therefore a fourth set of questions reflect some of their concerns that often are neglected in the design stage.

1. Does the design invite or discourage vandalism? Considerable research has been completed on this in recent years and good

design can reduce vandalism. Instead of the target-hardening approach, it may be both more economical and more effective to reduce the attractive opportunities for vandalism.[2]

2. Will it be possible and feasible to lock all doors except one on most weekday occasions?

3. Does the design include "zoning" the building for heating and cooling purposes?

4. How will temperature and humidity changes affect the organ? Can these be controlled?

5. Can the sewer and waterlines be serviced without tearing up the floors?

6. Does the parking area drain toward or away from the church building?

7. Does the design include provisions for expanding the building?

8. Does the design allow a major change in the Sunday morning schedule (such as adding another worship service) without creating serious disruptions for the music and educational programs?

9. Will the design permit future changes in program? In many states, for example, the design requirements for children's programming lasting more than three or four or five hours per day are more rigorous than for children's programming lasting less than two and one-half hours per day.

10. Do all interior doors have a clear opening of at least thirty-six inches? If not, how do you plan to move furniture from one room to another? What about wheelchair accessibility?

11. Does the design meet accessibility standards for persons with handicapping conditions?

12. Are the proposed colors for wall and carpets ones that will make dirt and debris highly visible?

13. Does the design include a storage space for outdoor tools and lawn mowers?

14. Is there a separate room for the custodian's *exclusive* use?

Financial Considerations

While it may not be within the jurisdiction of the self-appraisal committee, there are four questions on financing that new building that frequently are overlooked and deserve at least brief consideration.

1. Is it assumed that today's generation of members should pay for the new building or that the users should bear a substantial part of the cost? This is a major factor in determining the length of the mortgage.

2. Frequently it turns out that the first building-fund drive was actually a "practice" effort for a second and far more successful financial campaign. Many contributors make a larger gift in the second fund-raising effort than in the first.

A second part of this issue is that it often is easier to raise money for a new building while it is under construction than it is to pay off a mortgage.

As a result of these two patterns some congregations have been delighted with the results when they (a) planned and carried out a one-year capital funds campaign during the building planning stage and (b) conducted a larger campaign concurrently with the construction program.

Would this sequence be appropriate for your congregation?

3. Every generation of church members possesses an inclination to remodel the nest. This is a secondary argument in favor of a construction program designed to include two or three stages rather than a comprehensive effort that will meet all forseeable needs for the next decade or two. In general, new members tend to be more enthusiastic about helping pay for that which they had a voice in designing rather than to help pay off a mortgage incurred by an earlier generation of leaders. Does this pattern speak to your planning?

4. Hundreds of congregations have experienced a remarkable response with a capital funds appeal in which they asked members to contribute out of their accumulated savings (rather than to pledge a portion of their future income) for a building-fund program. The amount received in that type of program is in cash, or the equivalent, rather than in pledges. This has a particular appeal when interest rates are high, in congregations with many "winter visitors" and/or when there is broad-based support for the building program. Typically the amount received is somewhere between one-third and three times the annual budget of that congregation for operating expenses and benevolences.

Should this approach be considered in financing your new program?

The questions raised in this chapter are not offered as a complete checklist for the building planning committee. They are offered only to raise issues and concerns that often are overlooked in the conventional approach. They are offered as a supplement, not as a textbook on building planning. Some of them may be raised by the self-appraisal committee as it monitors the total life, ministry, and program of your congregation.

Notes

Introduction

1. For a provocative and interesting introduction to information theory see Jeremy Campbell, *Grammatical Man* (New York: Simon & Schuster, 1982).
2. An excellent introduction to sociobiology and the author's overall approach is Edward O. Wilson, *On Human Nature* (Cambridge, Mass.: Harvard University Press, 1978).
3. Walter Wink, *The Bible in Human Transformation* (Philadelphia: Fortress Press, 1973).
4. Paul Colinvaux, *The Fates of Nations* (New York: Simon & Schuster, 1980).
5. Donald A. Schon, *The Reflective Practitioner* (New York: Basic Books, Publishers, 1983).

Chapter One

1. For a system that classifies small churches by their social setting see Douglas Walrath, "Types of Small Congregations and Their Implications for Planning," in *Small Churches Are Beautiful*, ed. Jackson W. Carroll (New York: Harper & Row, Publishers, 1977), or Douglas Walrath, "Social Change and Local Churches: 1951-75," in *Understanding Church Growth and Decline: 1950-1978*, eds. Dean R. Hoge and David A. Roozen (New York: The Pilgrim Press, 1979), p. 253. For an appraisal of several different systems for the classification of churches, see Lyle E. Schaller, *Activating the Passive Church* (Nashville: Abingdon Press, 1981), pp. 17-39.
2. While the last census of churches in the United States was completed in 1926, a recent and admittedly incomplete study reported on the membership of 231,708 congregations in 111 church bodies in the United States. Bernard Quinn, et al., *Churches and Church Membership in the United States 1980* (Atlanta, Ga.: Glenmary Research Center, 1982). When an allowance is made for the congregations in the denominations that did not participate in that survey plus the huge number of Black, Asian, Hispanic, independent and sectarian churches plus the uncounted house churches that would not be included in such a survey, the number of Protestant congregations in the United States exceeds 375,000. The number of Protestant churches in Canada is estimated to be between 25,000 and 35,000. Every detailed study indicates that *at least* one-fourth of these congregations average fewer than 35 people in attendance at the principal weekly worship experience and that proportion probably is closer to one-third.
3. This point is made very clearly in Carl S. Dudley, *Making the Small Church Effective* (Nashville: Abingdon Press, 1977), pp. 71-74.

Chapter Two

1. In this discussion I am heavily indebted to insights gleaned from Richard A. Gabriel and Paul L. Savage, *Crisis in Command* (New York: Hill and Wang, 1978). This book should be required reading for every executive at all levels of the organizational structure of the denomination. The pioneering book from a

Protestant perspective on the dangers confronting the churches when they place an excessive emphasis on business methods is Richard G. Hutcheson, Jr., *Wheel Within Wheel* (Atlanta, Ga.: John Knox Press, 1979). See also James D. Anderson and Ezra Earl Jones, *The Management of Ministry* (New York: Harper & Row, Publishers, 1978), and Lyle E. Schaller, "Economy or Performance" in *Parish Planning* (Nashville: Abingdon Press, 1971), pp. 221-40.

2. Among other inconsistencies is the fact that the short time frame used in most goal-setting procedures is inconsistent with Reinhold Niebuhr's admonition, "Nothing worth doing is completed in one lifetime."

3. See Anthony Downs, *An Economic Theory of Democracy* (New York: Harper & Row, Publishers, 1957) for a rational approach to bureaucratic theory. For a brilliant critique of the doctrine of rationality in the business world see Thomas J. Peters and Robert H. Waterman, Jr., *In Search of Excellence* (New York: Harper & Row, Publishers, 1982), pp. 29-54.

4. For a delightful and lucid introduction to the changes in how entrepreneurial bureaucracies motivate workers, see Harry Levinson, *The Great Jackass Fallacy* (Cambridge, Mass.: Harvard University Graduate School of Business Administration, 1973).

5. For a ringing affirmation of the need for leadership in the churches, see Ernest T. Campbell, "They Also Serve Who Lead," *Pulpit Digest* (November-December 1979), 7-10.

6. Adapted from an essay by Kermit Johnson, "Ethical Issues of Military Leadership," 4 *Parameters* (1974), 35-39.

7. Quoted in James Fallows, *National Defense* (New York: Random House, 1981), p. 113.

8. For two excellent statements on leadership in non-profit and religious organizations, see Robert K. Greenleaf, *The Servant as Leader* (Peterborough, N.H.: Windy Row Press, 1973), and Speed B. Leas, *Leadership and Conflict* (Nashville: Abingdon Press, 1982).

9. For four different approaches to the responsibilities of a person engaged in a calling as contrasted to one following a career, see Richard A. Gabriel, *To Serve with Honor* (Westport, Conn.: Greenwood Press, 1982), pp. 78, 136-38; George W. Ball, *The Past Has Another Pattern* (New York: W. W. Norton & Co., 1982); Fallows, *National Defense*, pp. 114-23; and Lewis Thomas, *The Youngest Science* (New York: The Viking Press, 1983).

10. For a provocative, although somewhat one-sided account of the flourishing of the adversary concept in American culture during the 1960s and the more recent emergence of an intellectual opposition to the adversary culture, see Norman Podhoretz, "The Adversary Culture and the New Class," in *New Class?* ed. B. Bruce-Briggs (New York: McGraw-Hill, 1979), pp. 19-31. (For an excellent summary statement of the recent decline in adversary relationships between organized labor and management from a labor perspective, see Stephen Schlossberg, "Burying the Picket," *The Washington Monthly* [October 1982], 46-48.) See also Robert Reich, *The Next American Revolution* (New York: Times Books, 1983).

11. Is it possible for a professor to be engaged in a strike against the university? Or is that a concept with internal contradictions that make it an impossibility? One response is illustrated by the story that shortly after he had been chosen to become president of Columbia University, Dwight D. Eisenhower had a brief conversation with a small group of faculty members. At the close of the conversation General Eisenhower thanked the professors, adding that this was his first opportunity to talk with any of the employees of the university. One

of the professors responded by saying, "Sir, we are not employees of Columbia University. We are the university!"

Another answer to that central question is that if a university has been transformed into an entrepreneurial bureaucracy, it is logical and reasonable to expect the faculty members to conclude that they are involved in an adversarial relationship with that bureaucracy and have a right to strike.

Can a congregation "go on strike" against the policies or actions of the denomination? Can a minister "go out on strike"? Should lay employees of a denominational agency join a labor union?

12. For an elaboration of this concept, see Dudley, *Making the Small Church Effective*, pp. 71-74.

13. For strategies for use by the individual agent of intentional change, see Lyle E. Schaller, *The Change Agent* (Nashville: Abingdon Press, 1972), pp. 71-74.

14. Introductions to the subject can be found in such books as Paul H. Harrison, *Authority and Power in the Free Church Tradition* (Carbondale: Southern Illinois University Press, 1959); Hutcheson, *Wheel Within Wheel*; Lyle E. Schaller, *The Decision-Makers* (Nashville: Abingdon Press, 1974); Charles Hardy, *Gods of Management: Who They Are, How They Work and Why They Fail* (London: Pam Books, 1979); Roger A. Johnson, *Congregations as Nurturing Communities* (Philadelphia: Division for Parish Services, Lutheran Church in America, 1979); John E. Biersdorf, *Hunger for Experience* (New York: The Seabury Press, 1975); and David S. Schuller, Merton F. Strommen, and Milo L. Brekke, eds., *Ministry in America* (New York: Harper & Row, Publishers, 1980).

15. Three examples of research directed largely or entirely at public educational institutions that speak directly to the churches can be cited to illustrate this point. Perhaps the best is Roger G. Barker and Paul V. Gump, *Big School, Small School* (Stanford, Calif.: Stanford University Press, 1964). This is an exceptionally useful book for those interested in the impact of the size of an institution on human behavior patterns. A second is James G. Anderson, *Bureaucracy in Education* (Baltimore: Johns Hopkins University Press, 1968). This case study of a large metropolitan school system reveals the pressure of institutional forces to turn the school into an entrepreneurial bureaucracy and to tempt teachers to abandon classroom teaching for the greater rewards of a position in the bureaucratic system. Anderson also points out that the resistance to innovation tends to be greater in large and small schools than in medium-size schools. He also points out that (a) as size increases, the need for rules become more apparent, (b) the rules may be used to defend the bureaucrats and the institution against criticism, (c) the greater the reliance on rules to control behavior and performance, the more likely the floor of expectations will become a ceiling, and (d) the reliance on rules and regulations fosters an impersonal attitude by teachers and administrators toward the students.

Perhaps the most significant observation for the churches from Anderson's research is that the greater the drift toward a bureaucratic structure, the greater the probability that the classroom teachers and the bureaucratic structure will perceive one another as adversaries.

Those interested in denominational and/or congregational mergers will find useful insights in Jonathan A. Sher, ed., *Education in Rural America: A Reassessment of Conventional Wisdom* (Boulder, Colo.: Westview Press, 1977).

16. An excellent introduction for church leaders interested in exploiting the findings of research on military organizations is Gabriel and Savage, *Crisis*

in Command. Other books that merit study include Morris Janowitz, *The Professional Soldier* (New York: Free Press, 1971); Sam C. Sarkesian, *The Professional Army Soldier in a Changing Society* (Chicago: Nelson-Hall, 1975); David Halberstam, *The Best and the Brightest* (Greenwich, Conn.: Fawcett, 1972); William Hauser, *America's Army in Crisis* (Baltimore: Johns Hopkins University Press, 1973); Gabriel, *To Serve with Honor*; Sam C. Sarkesian, ed., *Combat Effectiveness* (Beverly Hills, Calif.: Sage Publications, 1980); and Fallows, *National Defense*. An outstanding critique from an insider's perspective is by the former Chairman of the Joint Chiefs of Staff, David C. Jones, "What's Wrong with Our Defense Establishment," *New York Times Magazine*, November 7, 1982, pp. 38ff.

17. For a pioneering and award-winning book on marketing that speaks to leaders of religious organizations, see Theodore Levitt, *Innovation in Marketing* (New York: McGraw-Hill, 1972).

18. Perhaps the most helpful writer for church leaders is Peter Drucker. Special mention should be made of three of his books: *Managing in Turbulent Times* (New York: Harper & Row, Publishers, 1980); *Management: Tasks, Responsibilities and Practices* (New York: Harper & Row, Publishers, 1974); and *The Changing World of the Executive* (New York: Times Book, 1982). Also very useful are Harry Levinson, *Organizational Diagnosis* (Cambridge, Mass.: Harvard University Press, 1972); Harry Levinson, *Executive* (Cambridge, Mass.: Harvard University Press, 1981); and Warren G. Bennis, *Changing Organizations* (New York: McGraw-Hill, 1966).

Chapter Three

1. Lloyd R. Bailey, *The Pentateuch* (Nashville, Abingdon Press, 1982).
2. The terminology for the dichotomy of ideological and behavioral types is drawn from an excellent research report: Roger A. Johnson, *Congregations as Nurturing Communities* (Philadelphia: Division for Parish Services, Lutheran Church in America, 1979), pp. 63-68. This study notes the tension between the writings of Paul and those of Matthew and James on this same point.
3. The story of a liberal ideological-type congregation is told in Jeffrey K. Hadden and Charles F. Longino, Jr., *Gideon's Gang: A Case Study of the Church in Social Action* (Philadelphia: United Church Press, 1974).
4. Johnson, *Congregations as Nurturing Communities*, pp. 23-24, 63.

Chapter Four

1. Why unchurched people choose to unite with a church, why they first attended a particular congregation, and why they returned and later joined that church are three different questions. A revealing inquiry into why unchurched people decide to go to church can be found in Edward A. Rauff, *Why People Join the Church* (New York: The Pilgrim Press, 1979). When asked why they first attended a particular congregation, the most common response from church shoppers, including those transferring their membership by letter from another congregation, is they were invited by a member. When asked why they came back a second time and subsequently joined that church, the most common response is "the friendliness of the people." Another, but radically different two-part classification system is used by Harold Lindsell, *The Battle of the Bible* (Grand Rapids, Mich.: The Zondervan Corp., 1978) and *The Bible in the Balance* (Grand Rapids, Mich.: The Zondervan Corp., 1979).
2. I am greatly indebted to a lecture given by James A. Sanders for sparking my thinking on this subject. For his perspective, see James A. Sanders, *God Has a Story, Too* (Philadelphia: Fortress Press, 1979).

Chapter Five

1. For suggestions for the agenda when a pulpit search committee and a candidate meet for an interview, see Robert G. Kemper, *Beginning a New Pastorate* (Nashville: Abingdon Press, 1978), pp. 30-89, and Lyle E. Schaller, *The Pastor and the People* (Nashville: Abingdon Press, 1973), pp. 16-64.

Chapter Eight

1. For historical data on church attendance patterns, see Martin E. Marty, et al., *What Do We Believe?* (New York: Meredith Press, 1968), pp. 212-13, and Joseph Veroff, et al., *The Inner American* (New York: Basic Books, Publishers, 1981), pp. 454-69. See also the annual Gallup Polls on church attendance by age and gender.
2. For an excellent analysis of these patterns of change see Dean R. Hoge, *Converts, Dropouts, Returnees: A Study of Religious Change Among Catholics* (New York: The Pilgrim Press, 1981).
3. Robert S. Lynch and Helen M. Lynd, *Middletown: A Study in American Culture* (New York: Harcourt and Brace Jovanovich, 1929).
4. For a brief introduction to this subject see Jim Fowler and Sam Keen, *Life Maps* (Waco: Word Books, 1978) or Mary M. Wilcox, *Developmental Journey* (Nashville: Abingdon Press, 1979) or Jack Renard Pressau, *I'm Saved, You're Saved . . . Maybe* (Atlanta, Ga.: John Knox Press, 1977). For a more exhaustive statement see James W. Fowler, *The Psychology of Human Development and the Quest for Meaning* (New York: Harper & Row, Publishers, 1981). The United Methodist Church offers a curriculum series *Ages and Stages* that is based on the concept of adult faith development.
5. In 1924 there was one church building in Muncie, Indiana, for every 860 residents compared to one for every 585 residents in 1978 when the frequency of church attendance among Muncie residents was approximately double what it had been in 1924. Theodore Caplon, et al., *Middletown Families* (Minneapolis: University of Minnesota Press, 1982), pp. 251, 385.
6. For some speculation on how the churches are oriented toward women, rather than men, and for suggestions on how to reverse that trend, see Lyle E. Schaller, "Where Have All the Men Gone?" *Presbyterian Survey* (September 1982), 19-21.

Chapter Nine

1. Nearly all of the literature in this field is directed at the value of small groups. Very little is available on the distinctive role of large groups in the churches. For a summary of much of the research on small group dynamics, see A. Paul Hare, *Handbook of Small Group Research*, 2nd. ed. (New York: The Free Press, 1976). For suggestions on large group dynamics, see Dick Murray, *Strengthening the Adult Sunday School Class* (Nashville: Abingdon Press, 1981), and Lyle E. Schaller, *Effective Church Planning* (Nashville: Abingdon Press, 1979), pp. 17-64.
2. The disappearance of social class distinctions as a distinctive characteristic of Protestant congregations is a major theme in Caplow, et al., *Middletown Families*.
3. For a more extensive discussion of these exceptions, see Lyle E. Schaller, *Assimilating New Members* (Nashville: Abingdon Press, 1978), pp. 24-35.
4. These congregations are described in greater detail, with suggestions on changing from a passive to an active role, in Schaller, *Activating the Passive Church*.

Chapter Ten

1. For an elaboration of this point see Schaller, *Assimilating New Members*, pp. 69-98.

Chapter Twelve

1. For other resources and criteria in evaluating the youth program in your church, see Steve Clapp and Jerry O. Cook, *Youth Workers' Handbook* (Sidell, Ill.: C-4 Resources, 1981); Wayne Rice, *Junior High Ministry* (Grand Rapids, Mich: The Zondervan Corp., 1978); Glenn E. Ludwig, *Building an Effective Youth Ministry* (Nashville: Abingdon Press, 1979); and Lyle E. Schaller, "Looking at Youth Ministries," in *Survival Tactics in the Parish* (Nashville: Abingdon Press, 1977), pp. 144-54.

Chapter Thirteen

1. For two very provocative statements on what is being taught, see Benson R. Snyder, *The Hidden Curriculum* (New York: Alfred A. Knopf, 1971) and Egil Peterson, et al., "A New Perspective on the Effects of First-Grade Teachers on Children's Subsequent Adult Status," *Harvard Educational Review*, 48 (February 1978), 1-31.

Chapter Fourteen

1. For questions on this issue see *Accessibility Audit for Churches* (Prepared by Health and Welfare Division, General Board of Global Ministries, The United Methodist Church, 1981). For a more comprehensive response to the churches' ministry with the handicapped, see Harold H. Wilke, *Creating the Caring Congregation* (Nashville: Abingdon Press, 1980).

2. An introduction to this concept can be found in Gerald D. Suttles, *The Social Construction of Communities* (Chicago: University of Chicago Press, 1972). See also James Wise, "A Gentle Deterrent to Vandalism," *Psychology Today* (September 1982), 31-38.